EK-KLĀ-SĒ'-Ä

A CALL TO RETURN TO NEW TESTAMENT CHRISTIANITY

"Its Faith and Practice"

Tim Cocklin - CCF

If you feel you cannot afford the cost of the book, all the publications authored by Tim Cocklin are available to anyone on a donation basis. You will be sent a copy regardless of the amount offered. You must, however, order it from us directly. On-line retailers are not subject to our policy. For instructions on how to obtain a copy send an email to:
ekklasea @worldsofwonderpublishing.com

EK-KLĀ-SĒ'-Ä-

A CALL TO RETURN TO NEW TESTAMENT CHRISTIANITY
"Its Faith and Practice"

© 2014 Worlds of Wonder Publishing
Dallas, Texas

ISBN-13: 978-1502369963
ISBN-10: 1502369966

Unless otherwise indicated, Scripture is taken from the King James Version for reasons of copyright.

Unless otherwise stated all quotes from the early church fathers are taken from public domain books from the Christian Classics Ethereal Library. Their website link is: www.ccel.org

World rights reserved. No part of this publication may be stored in a retrieval system, reproduced, or transmitted in any way or by any means — electronic, mechanical, photocopy, magnetic recording, or any other — without the prior written permission of the publisher.

Address all correspondence to:
ekklasea @worldsofwonderpublishing.com

Second Edition November 2014

Dedication:

This book is dedicated to my father in the faith William Gay. His love and devotion to the Lord inspired many in the faith. To Shirley his wife and my mother in the faith. Her service to mankind cannot be surpassed. Although Bill is enjoying his new life with the Lord, Shirley continues even today to be an example of faith, service and hospitality wherever she goes. May this book bring honor to them and the Lord.

To Genie Hocking Nickerson for her hospitality, genuine care and love for people regardless of their standing in life. Shirley and Genie are both examples for us to follow as New Testament believers.

To my wife, Cindy, who continued to support and encourage me to finish the book, who corrected many of the typing errors and made many suggestions. Without her help and support I would not be able to do half the things I have done.

Acknowledgments:

Special thanks to Denise Wright and Shirley Gay
for proof reading, corrections and support.

Warning:

This book will offend and disturb some. It is not my intent to be purposefully offensive, however, I have endeavored to stay away from the traditions of man as much as possible in an attempt to get a clear picture of the New Testament Church and this many times will go against traditional thought. I expect that many will disagree with what I am writing. People do not like change of any kind. To suggest that something is out of order is disturbing to many people. Going against the established order can be dangerous as any reformer knows. We have drifted so far from the original New Testament Way that the apostles would not recognize the ek-klā-sē'-ä today. As the church follows the world into apostasy we must stand up as watchmen on the wall and blow the alarm.

I request that you search the scriptures for yourself and come to your own conclusions. My purpose is to find out what made the early church so effective and why our churches today have become so ineffective.

I blame the structure of the church for many of the problems we have today; not equipping the saints and making a religion out of a relationship.

Contents

	Introduction to the ek-klā-sē'-ä	1
Section 1 -	Membership in the ek-klā-sē'-ä	13
Section 2 -	Purpose of the ek-klā-sē'-ä	33
Section 3 -	Leadership in the ek-klā-sē'-ä	47
Section 4 -	Operation of the ek-klā-sē'-ä	95
Section 5 -	History of the ek-klā-sē'-ä	133
	Appendix A: Resources	161

> "The Christianity of the New Testament simply does not exist… what has to be done is to throw light upon a criminal offense against Christianity prolonged through centuries, perpetrated by millions (more or less guiltily), whereby they have cunningly, under the guise of perfecting Christianity, sought little by little to cheat God out of Christianity and have succeeded in making Christianity exactly the opposite of what it is in the New Testament"
>
> *Attack Upon Christendom*
> Kirkegaard, 1956

> The word ekklesia appears in the Greek text where this word is found in the translations. ekklesia comes from Kaleo "to call," and ek "out from." The compound verb means "to call out from." In classical Greek ekklesia referred to an assembly of the citizens summoned by the town crier. It is used in Acts 19:32-41 in its purely classical meaning. - Kenneth Wuest - Wuest's Word Studies of the New Testament[1]

Introduction

All around us we find Christians who are totally defeated, without hope, ineffectual and wounded. It appears that evil is winning in every avenue of life. People are leaving the church in droves. Where is the victory? Where is the power? Where is the true church? Where is the burning desire to evangelize? The salt of the earth has lost its savor, its drive and its power. What happened to this once powerful force which changed the world? Today's churches have the form but no power. The church has been lulled into a deep sleep of apathy and self-indulgence. It is time to wakeup and restore what remains before we are diluted to the point where no one can tell the difference between Christians and the world! We must fall on our faces and cry out to the Lord and beg for a great revival of the remnant.

We find over and over in the Old Testament the twelve tribes would begin to fall away and start serving other gods. The Lord would in turn allow trouble to follow. When things got bad enough they would turn back to the Lord for help. In His mercy God would restore them. This was a continuous cycle of turning away then turning back. Today's church has turned away from the Lord. We must find our way back to the Lord who bought us and restore the walls that have been torn down by self-righteousness and pride. We must humble ourselves under the mighty hand of God.

> *Humble yourselves therefore under the mighty hand of God, that he may exalt you in due time: Casting all your care upon him; for he careth for you. Be sober, be vigilant; because your adversary the devil, as a roaring lion, walketh about, seeking whom he may devour: 1 Peter 5:6-8 (KJV)*

It is not necessary that we be strong on our own, for the Lord told Paul that His strength is made complete in our weakness. Kenneth Wuest translates 2 Corinthians 12:6 most accurately:

> *And He has said to me, and His declaration still stands, My grace is enough for you, for power is moment by moment coming to its full energy and complete operation in the sphere of weakness. Therefore, most gladly will I the rather boast in my weaknesses in order that the power of the Christ may take up its residence in me . Wherefore I am well content in weaknesses, in insults, in necessities, in persecutions, and in circumstances under which I am subject to extreme pressure on behalf of Christ, for when I am weak, then I am filled with ability and power. 2 Corinthians 12:6 (WuestNT[1])*

We must be in the habit of putting our full trust in the Lord and not our own cleverness or strength. Victory is the Lord's if we will but stand by and see the salvation of the Lord.

> *Ye shall not need to fight in this battle: set yourselves, stand ye still, and see the salvation of the Lord with you, O Judah and Jerusalem: fear not, nor be dismayed; tomorrow go out against them: for the Lord will be with you. 2 Chronicles 20:17 (KJV)*

It would be foolish to claim that anyone (except the Holy Spirit) has all the answers concerning how the church of today should operate. However, it is

EK-KLĀ-SĒ'-Ä - Introduction

critical that we separate tradition from truth. This document is a study on what a New Testament fellowship might look like and how it might operate today. The beliefs expressed here come from over forty years of studying the Word and from observing the operation of churches and fellowships. I have researched this subject for a long time and to the best of my ability I am passing what I have learned on to the reader. We are all fallible so I suggest that you search the scriptures yourself and come to your own conclusion. Hopefully, this book will stir you enough that you will seek the guidance of the Holy Spirit and the written Word.

The first thing to realize is that there is a difference between being a member of the body of Christ and being a member of a local church the ἐκκλησία ek-klā-sē'-ä: (an assembly of the people or what is commonly referred to as the church). The word means "called out ones" and carries with it the idea of gathering together. Being a member of the body of Christ occurs at new birth; neither baptism nor signing a membership card can make you a member of this austere group, although some would have us believe that it does. Being a member of a local ek-klā-sē'-ä simply means attending a local gathering of believers. Contrary to common practice today, there is no New Testament concept of membership in a local church other than attendance. On the other hand, all denominations and hierarchical structures are man-made designed to control what happens with the membership under its control; what they believe and how they operate their churches. In the New Testament local oversight is made up of first the headship of Christ; second, the guidance of the Holy Spirit and third, by mature elders and deacons with definite and very distinct qualifications, which is not followed in today's fellowships.

In the late 1960's and early 1970's, there was an outpouring of the Holy Spirit. As the Spirit moved across the United States thousands of young people and even those in traditional denominations were swept into the Kingdom of God. Groups were formed without denominational ties. In some cases, fellowships sprang up within denominational churches. In many of these cases the rouge groups were asked to leave the church building since they were in disagreement with the established order of the denomination. Young people were voraciously hungry to know the Savior. These young people, myself included were from the hippie/drug culture of the time, long hair, ragged clothes, but willing and eager to break with

EK-KLĀ-SĒ'-Ä - Introduction

traditional beliefs. Others in traditional churches, being influenced by the Holy Spirit, began to question what they believed. They had a desire to seek a deeper walk with their Lord. We knew that it was a move of the Holy Spirit because as we would speak to believers in different parts of the country, they would echo back to us what we had also heard from the Lord confirming what the Spirit was saying at the time. We must remember that just because the Holy Spirit was saying something then, The Spirit may be bringing new emphasis today. The Logos never changes but the move of the Spirit may be different from time to time. We must not try to reenact what once was unless it is Spirit lead. This is was causes people to fabricate a move of the Spirit where there is none. Our relationship must be living in a daily relationship with our Lord or suffer stagnation. In the Old Testament the Israelites were told to use running water we should have a fresh filling of the Holy Spirit daily. (More on that in the chapter on operations).

During this time period there was a great unity, but little or no formal organization among those who followed the leading of the Spirit. There was a genuine hunger to know the truth. Although, it was not many years later when the enemy started sowing seeds of doubt, unbelief and disunity into this newly, but very loosely formed group. Where there was once freedom, bondage and manmade rules began to creep in. The enthusiasm began to wane and religion replaced relationship. When this begins to happen, rules become the order of the day. Where religious structure and men begin to rule, the Holy Spirit is pushed out in favor of control. It is then that the Messiah is replaced as head of the church and man feels like he must control the group. You could see this happen in the Reformation, and in all mighty moves of God. Further we see false miracles and a forced version of the move of the Spirit. This is where there is a form or pattern of what the Holy Spirit used to do but now is man's effort to recreate a move of the Spirit. The spark that got the fire going soon goes out and what is left is mostly fabricated.

It is during these times when the Lord is silent that we need to fall on our faces before God and plead for him to come and meet with us. Coming up with new programs to create excitement is a mistake. Yet, that is exactly what we see today. One of the most dangerous trends we see is when churches use secular marketing and management techniques to grow their congregations. Does it work? Yes, we see some churches grow astronomically. But at what cost? What is the purpose of these mega churches? Are they truly discipling their people? I am very weary of mega congregations because Yeshua tells us *"The way is narrow and there are few who find it"*. When you see mass numbers of people following a man or an organization, beware! Unless there is a current move of the Holy Spirit universally, like we have seen in past revivals, then the growth seen in these mega organizations is manufactured by man and will not stand when the winds blow. Why? Because it is not on the solid foundation of Yeshua Ha Meschiach, Jesus the Messiah.

We must become like Esther, who before going on her mission took the matter very seriously and fasted three days before going before the king. We should be willing to wait upon the Lord and not run ahead of Him. All activity, even though it may appear to be "good", may not be the plan and purpose of God at this moment in time. We must find the pillar and the cloud and move when He moves.

If God goes before us we will have the victory, if not then it is all vain glory and death soon follows. Death in this sense fortunately does not mean the non-existence of the entity known as the church but death in the sense that victory is not often found, things are dry and fruitless. We can see from the Old Testament that if the King first sought the Lord and obeyed his command then victory was sure. If the king did not seek the Lord defeat was sure to follow.

Take for example King Asa of the southern kingdom of Judah. Zerah the Ethiopian went to war against him at Mareshah and he was out numbered two to one or more.

> *Asa cried out to the Lord his God, telling him, "Lord, there is no one except for you to help between the powerful and the weak. So help us, Lord God, because we're depending on you and have come against this vast group in your name. Lord, you are our God. Let no mere mortal man defeat you! So the Lord defeated the Ethiopians right in front of Asa and Judah, and the Ethiopians ran away.*
> 2 Chronicles 14:11

It was a great victory and they carried off great wealth. Upon their return Asa is given a warning :

EK-KLĀ-SĒ'-Ä - Introduction

> *After this, the Spirit of God came to rest on Oded's son Azariah, so he went out to meet Asa and rebuked him: "Listen to me, Asa, Judah, and Benjamin! The Lord is with you when you are with him. If you seek him, he will allow you to find him, but if you abandon him, he will abandon you. 2 Chronicles 15:1,2*

Then, years later, we read about Asa's fear how the King of the northern kingdom came against him. He made a monstrous mistake and put his trust in man for his help instead of the Lord.

> *During the thirty- sixth year of Asa's reign, King Baasha of Israel invaded Judah and interdicted Ramah by building fortifications around it so no one could enter or leave to join King Asa of Judah. But Asa removed some silver and gold from the treasuries of the Lord's Temple and from his royal palace and sent them to King Ben- hadad of Aram, who lived in Damascus. 2 Chronicles 16:1-2*

This time Asa did not inquire of the Lord and the seer came and rebuked him and reminds him of the victory the Lord gave him against the Ethiopians He then predicts what will happen as a result of his actions. From then on they will have war in the kingdom of Judah.

> *Right about then, Hanani the seer came to King Asa of Judah and rebuked him. "Because you have put your trust in the king of Aram and have not relied on the Lord your God, the army of the king of Aram has escaped from your control. Weren't the Ethiopians and the Libyans a vast army with many chariots and cavalry? Yet because you relied on the Lord, he gave them into your control! The Lord's eyes keep on roaming throughout the earth, looking for those whose hearts completely belong to him, so that he may strongly support them. But because you have acted foolishly in this, from now on you will have wars.". 2 Chronicles 16:7-9*

In the beginning Asa did what was right before the Lord by tearing down the high places, idol worship, and commanding Judah to seek the Lord. But you can clearly see that when difficult times come we must turn to the Lord and inquire of His will. This is not time to come up with new programs or depend on our own cleverness to resolve issues. If the blessing and the peace of God has been lifted, this is the time to seek God. This is how churches become dead, lukewarm and worthless because the answer came from their own cleverness not from the Lord.

We must learn from Asa that the Lord wants us to seek Him for answers He does <u>NOT</u> expect us to find our own answer as Asa did in contacting King Ben-Hadad. The old adage "God helps those who help themselves" is a lie from our enemy to deceive us into trusting in ourselves. We will suffer defeat whenever we rely on our own or the help of man. I want to give you a warning from Jeremiah:

The Curse of Trusting in mankind:

Thus saith the Lord; Cursed be the man that trusteth in man, and maketh flesh his arm, and whose heart departeth from the Lord.

For he shall be like the heath in the desert, and shall not see when good cometh; but shall inhabit the parched places in the wilderness, in a salt land and not inhabited.

The Blessing of Trusting the Lord:

Blessed is the man that trusteth in the Lord, and whose hope the Lord is. For he shall be as a tree planted by the waters, and that spreadeth out her roots by the river, and shall not see when heat cometh, but her leaf shall be green; and shall not be careful in the year of drought, neither shall cease from yielding fruit.

> *The fear of man bringeth a snare: but whoso putteth his trust in the Lord shall be safe.*
> Proverbs 29:25

The heart is deceitful above all things, and desperately wicked: who can know it? I the Lord search the heart, I try the reins, even to give every man according to his ways, and according to the fruit of his doings. Jeremiah 17:5-11

I can tell you first hand that during those times where I trusted in my own cleverness and intelligence the end result was disastrous. I paid for those mistakes for years afterwards. However, when I waited upon the Lord for guidance and direction, trusting totally in him the outcome was always good.

It is our duty as members of the body of Christ to put our faith and trust completely in the Lord not in a pastor, an organization, people or ourselves. They will all fail you, disappoint you and generally make a mess of things. We must each individually rely on the Lord. We must as Yeshua said in Matthew 6 *"Seek the Lord first"*. If you find yourself in a dry place your first question should be "am I trusting in man, myself or the Lord?" The answer may reveal why you are under a curse or in a dry place. Remember the heart is deceitful and desperately wicked, trust only in the Lord and his word and be blessed...

The seven churches of Revelation should be a clue to us about what the Lord thinks about self-reliance.

> *I know what you've been doing. You are known for being alive, but you are dead. Be alert, and strengthen the things that are left, which are about to die. I note that your actions are incomplete before my God. Revelation 3:1*

> *And Since you are lukewarm and neither hot nor cold, I am going to spit you out of my mouth. You say, "I am rich. I have become wealthy. I don't need anything." Yet you don't realize that you are miserable, pitiful, poor, blind, and naked. Therefore, I advise you to buy from me gold purified in fire so you may be rich, white clothes to wear so your shameful nakedness won't show, and ointment to put on your eyes so you may see. I correct and discipline those whom I love, so be serious and repent! Rev 3:16-19*

Our first duty when things begin to get quiet or when we see the blessing of the Lord slip away, is to diligently seek the Lord and His direction. The story of Asa should be a lesson for us. When Hanani the seer told Asa that *"The Lord's eyes keep on roaming throughout the earth, looking for those whose hearts completely belong to him, so that he may strongly support them"* we should take it seriously. Looking for our own solution is the first step towards being dead like the church of Sardis or worse being spewed out of the Lord's mouth like the Laodiceans.

EK-KLĀ-SĒ'-Ä - Introduction

You will find that throughout the New Testament that the word ek-klā-sē'-ä (church) is singular except in cases where a region is referred. I realize that in large cities it would be virtually impossible for all Christians in that area to meet in one place. However, because there are factions and disagreements we have Baptist churches, Lutheran Churches and a multitude of others. Paul tells us that God gave us functions within the body so that we could come to a unity of faith and spiritual maturity.

> *And he gave some, apostles; and some, prophets; and some, evangelists; and some, pastors and teachers; For the perfecting of the saints, for the work of the ministry, for the edifying of the body of Christ: Till we all come in the unity of the faith, and of the knowledge of the Son of God, unto a perfect man, unto the measure of the stature of the fullness of Christ: That we henceforth be no more children, tossed to and fro, and carried about with every wind of doctrine, by the sleight of men, and cunning craftiness, whereby they lie in wait to deceive; But speaking the truth in love, may grow up into him in all things, which is the head, even Christ: From whom the whole body fitly joined together and compacted by that which every joint supplieth, according to the effectual working in the measure of every part, maketh increase of the body unto the edifying of itself in love. Ephesians 4:11-16 (KJV)*

If you were to observe our assemblies today you would say that this august group had failed in its mission.

The last sections of this book will deal with the history of the church from the early days of the apostles until today. History clearly shows the strategies used by the enemy to distract and distort truth. Because of this deception the church has become increasingly ineffective and for the most part fruitless.

It is clear that even at the early stages of the church that Satan's influence was having a great effect even before Edict of Milan issued by Constantine which made Christianity an official Roman religion in 313 AD. Sometimes the best defense against a movement is to diffuse it with acceptance and then control it. This is exactly what Satan did through Constantine. A direct result of this was a period of time known as the dark ages where truth was replaced with lies and deception. The church controlled what was taught. The Word of God was not available to the common man. This meant that the church could teach whatever it wanted. From this came the indulgences and the Inquisition.

If you want to know the future, look at the past - Jacob Prasch (http://www.moriel.org) What happen in Acts will happen again in the last days, both the outpouring of the Holy Spirit and the persecution. That means that the true ek-klā-sē'-ä will come under persecution from religious organizations and secular humanists. Our belief that deviant behaviors should not be allowed in the fellowship is coming under hostile fire. This persecution will cause true Christians to come together and leave their differences behind. Christianity is increasingly coming under fire and in many ways is being outlawed. Subtlety they chip away at our freedoms in the name of hate crimes and other lies. And the people will follow the false prophets and teachers in to the ä-po-stä-sē'-ä apostasy (falling away).

> *Let no man deceive you by any means: for that day shall not come, except there come a **falling away [G646]** first, and that man of sin be revealed, the son of perdition; 2 Thessalonians 2:3*

> Strong's G646: falling away: a defection, revolt, apostasy, is used in the NT of religious apostasy; in Act 21:21, it is translated "to forsake," lit., "thou teachest apostasy from Moses." In 2Th 2:3 "the falling away" signifies apostasy from the faith. In papyri documents it is used politically of rebels. Vines Dictionary of New Testament Words[2]

> *I marvel that ye are so soon removed from him that called you into the grace of Christ unto another gospel: Which is not another; but there be some that trouble you, and would pervert the gospel of Christ. But though we, or an angel from heaven, preach any other gospel unto you than that which we have preached unto you, let him be accursed. As we said before, so say I now again, If any man preach any other gospel unto you than that ye have received, let him be accursed. Galatians 1:6-9 (KJV)*

EK-KLĀ-SĒ'-Ä - Introduction

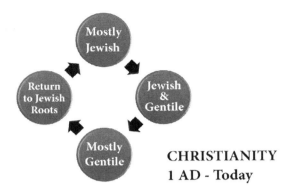

CHRISTIANITY
1 AD - Today

We have come full circle, from a totally Jewish Christianity, to a Gentile Christianity and now we are seeing a movement to return to our Jewish roots. As always, some go overboard and want to bring us back under the law by strictly observing the Sabbath and other ceremonial requirements even adult circumcision. We must be cautious not to get caught up in that. We should, however, learn what true New Testament Christianity is and rediscover our Jewish roots.

1. Word Studies from the Greek New Testament (4 volume set) Kenneth S. Wuest
   Publisher: William B. Eerdmans Publishing Company

2. Vine's Complete Expository Dictionary of Old and New Testament Words
   by W. E. Vine Publisher: Thomas Nelson

"But the love of money is the root of all evils." Knowing, therefore, that "as we brought nothing into the world, so we can carry nothing out," let us arm ourselves with the armour of righteousness; and let us teach, first of all, ourselves to walk in the commandments of the Lord. Next, [teach] your wives [to walk] in the faith given to them, and in love and purity tenderly loving their own husbands in all truth, and loving all [others] equally in all chastity; and to train up their children in the knowledge and fear of God. Teach the widows to be discreet as respects the faith of the Lord, praying continually for all, being far from all slandering, evil-speaking, false-witnessing, love of money, and every kind of evil; knowing that they are the altar of God, that He clearly perceives all things, and that nothing is hid from Him, neither reasonings, nor reflections, nor any one of the secret things of the heart.

The Epistle of Polycarp to the Philippians Chapter IV.—Various exhortations. Polycarp

1

Membership

EK-KLĀ-SĒ'-Ä - Membership

Nowhere in the New Testament do we find the requirement for formal membership in a local congregation. That is not to say that I think it is wrong except for what the motivation is for such a requirement. Where the word is silent we must not assume or read into it what we want it to say. There is no place for allegiance to an organization our only allegiance should be to the Lord himself.

However, we need to have a commitment to each other. We need to be aware of the needs of our brothers and sisters. I don't believe necessarily that Christians should live communally (unless the Lord, not some cult leader, tells you to). I do not think that we should sell everything and give it all to the poor (unless the Lord tells you to do so). We should have an awareness of the needs of others. The Word does tell us to be especially aware of orphans and widows:

> *Pure religion and undefiled before God and the Father is this, To visit the fatherless and widows in their affliction, and to keep himself unspotted from the world.* James 1:27

Be a good steward of the money God has given you. If you want to seed into a ministry, seed into your local fellowship. Meet the needs of the poor and needy locally so you will know where the money is being spent or with organizations that will tell you exactly were each dime is spent. Always remember those who are sent out as missionaries especially if they are sent out from your fellowship. There are ministries who spend so much on advertising and administration that your gift is reduced by 50% or even more and only a very small percentage of your gift ever gets to the purpose stated by the ministry. There is not much of a return on investment for organizations and preachers which are not transparent and there are plenty of those who will take your money. The charlatans will keep a large portion of the money and spend it on lavish live styles stating

> *For the scripture saith, Thou shalt not muzzle the ox that treadeth out the corn. And, The labourer is worthy of his reward.*
> 1 Timothy 5:18

I would beware of such ministries. Many of these people have become wealthy at the expense of innocent Christians. It is not wrong to be wealthy it is wrong to beg for money when the intent is to amass fortunes while misrepresenting its intended purpose.

Is there a building where the ekklāsē'ä are to meet?

> For every dollar of money spent to minister to the poor, the typical American church spends more than five dollars on buildings and maintenance. George Barna, *The Second Coming of the Church* -Word Publishing, pg. 3

I cannot find a requirement for having a building in the New Testament. Yes, it is true that they met in the Jewish temple on Saturdays but the early Christians were all Jews so that would be expected. We are also told that they met from house to house. Remember how Eutychus fell asleep while Paul was preaching in an upper chamber.

> *And upon the first day of the week, when the disciples came together to break bread, Paul preached unto them, ready to depart on the morrow; and continued his speech until midnight. And there were many lights in the upper chamber, where they were gathered together. And there sat in a window a certain young man named Eutychus, being fallen into a deep sleep: and as Paul was long preaching, he sunk down with sleep, and fell down from the third loft, and was taken up dead.*
> Acts 20:7-9 (KJV)

And Peter having been set free from jail by an angel comes to a meeting at Mary's house:

> *And when he had considered the thing, he came to the house of Mary the mother of John, whose surname was Mark; where many were gathered together praying. And as Peter knocked at the door of the gate, a damsel came to hearken, named Rhoda. And when she knew Peter's voice, she opened not the gate for gladness, but ran in, and told how Peter stood before the gate. And they said unto her, Thou art mad. But she constantly affirmed that it was even so. Then said they, It is his angel. But Peter continued knocking: and when they had opened the door, and saw him, they were astonished.*
> Acts 12:12-16 (KJV)

As persecution continues to rise in the United States we can expect that true believers will out of necessity meet in private homes. At the time of this writing we are already seeing traditional churches turn from the bible to accept changes in the culture. Because of their acceptance of cultural evolution we can expect that the organized church will also persecute true Christians that strictly follow the Word without compromise.

> *A little leaven leaveneth the whole lump.*
> **Galatians 5:9**

There is a growing hatred for Christians and what we believe from the Word of God. Unless a very large revival comes to this once great nation we will see the end of religious freedom as we know it today. It is already being eroded by the so called "hate crimes" and other groups hell bent on the eradication of Christianity. True Christians do not hate sinners we just don't accept their sin according to the scripture.

If it is analyzed honestly the exact opposite of this hate is true they hate us for our beliefs which do not accept their sin. We are all sinners, true Christians will repent and turn from sin once it is realized. That does not make us better, only forgiven. We cannot accept open sin in our fellowships whether it be adultery, homosexuality or whatever the Word warns us against. Paul tells us in Ephesians not to have fellowship with those who practice such things.

> "Fellowship" is sunkoinōneō, "to become a partaker together with others." The word refers to a joint-participation between two or more individuals in a common interest and a common activity. Wuest's Word Studies[1]

But fornication, and all uncleanness, or covetousness, let it not be once named among you, as becometh saints; Neither filthiness, nor foolish talking, nor jesting, which are not convenient: but rather giving of thanks. For this ye know, that no whoremonger, nor unclean person, nor covetous man, who is an idolater, hath any inheritance in the kingdom of Christ and of God. Let no man deceive you with vain words: for because of these things cometh the wrath of God upon the children of disobedience. Be not ye therefore

> *partakers with them. For ye were sometimes darkness, but now are ye light in the Lord: walk as children of light: (For the fruit of the Spirit is in all goodness and righteousness and truth;) Proving what is acceptable unto the Lord. And have no fellowship with the unfruitful works of darkness, but rather reprove them. For it is a shame even to speak of those things which are done of them in secret. Ephesians 5:3-12 (KJV)*

Paul just mentioned several types of acts and manners that are unacceptable to Christians and tells the Ephesians not to have fellowship with them.

In verse 12 we are told not to talk about their deeds. Alfred's Greek New Testament Commentary[2] quotes Devar Klotz: the connexion being—'I mention not, and you need not speak of, these deeds of darkness, much less have any fellowship with them—your connexion with them must be only that which the act of ἔλεγξις necessitates')

Today there is a lot of controversy about whether or not these acts are actually sin or not. Mainline denominations are readily accepting this sin into their congregations. If we look back to the Ante-Nicene teachings the fathers who were around in the first three centuries we find the following:

Homosexuality and pederasty

> The Didache (di dah KAY) AD 100, a commentary on the gospels item 2.2: You shall not commit adultery; you shall not commit pederasty.

> Pederasty: "Thou shalt not seduce young boys."
> Barry Coldrey book, *Religious Life Without Integrity*, 2002, P & B Press, page 27.

> In like manner, let the young men also be blameless in all things, being especially careful to preserve purity, and keeping themselves in, as with a bridle, from every

kind of evil. For it is well that they should be cut off from the lusts that are in the world, since "every lust warreth against the spirit; " and "**neither fornicators, nor effeminate**, nor **abusers of themselves with mankind**, shall inherit the kingdom of God," nor those who do things inconsistent and unbecoming. Polycarp, AD 120 *Epistle of Polycarp* 5:3

the whole earth has now become full of fornication and wickedness. I admire the ancient legislators of the Romans: these detested **effeminacy of conduct; and *the giving of the body to feminine purposes***, contrary to the law of nature, they judged worthy of the extremest penalty, according to the righteousness of the law. Clement Of Alexandria *Instructor Chapter III.—Against Men Who Embellish Themselves.*

I should suppose the coupling of two males to be a very shameful thing, or else the one must be a female, and so the male is discredited by the female. Tertullian, AD 197 - *Against the Valentinians Chapter XI.*

There are many other references concerning homosexuality by the very early church fathers, suffice it to say that it was NOT accepted by the early church or New testament scriptures and neither should we.

Another sin creeping into our fellowships is abortion. This is not a new practice it was around during the first centuries.

Abortion

thou shalt not murder a child by abortion nor kill them when born - *The Didache or Teaching of the Apostles* 2:2

Thou shalt not slay the child by procuring abortion; nor, again, shalt thou destroy it after it is born. - Chapter XIX.—*The way of light - the Epistle of Barnabas*

But Christians now are so far from homicide, that with them it is utterly unlawful to make away a child in the womb, when nature is in deliberation about the man; for to kill a child before it is born is to commit murder by way of advance; and there is no difference whether you destroy a child in its formation, or after it is formed and delivered. For we Christians look upon him as a man, who is one in embryo; for he is in being, like the fruit in blossom, and in a little time would have been a perfect man, had nature met with no disturbance. *Tertullian's Apology for the Christians.*

How, then, is a living being conceived? Is the substance of both body and soul formed together at one and the same time? Or does one of them precede the other in natural formation? We indeed maintain that both are conceived, and formed, and perfectly simultaneously, as well as born together; and that not a moment's interval occurs in their conception, so that, a prior place can be assigned to either. - *Tertullian's A Treatise on the Soul Chapter 27.*

How, then, when we do not even look on, lest we should contract guilt and pollution, can we put people to death? **And when we say that those women who use drugs to bring on abortion commit murder, and will have to give an account to God or the abortion,** on what principle should we commit murder? For it does not belong to the same person to regard the very foetus in the womb as a created being, and therefore an object of God's care, and when it has passed into life, to kill it; and not to expose an infant, because those who expose them are chargeable with child-murder, and on the other hand, when it has been reared to destroy it. *A plea for the Christians* - By Athenagoras the Athenian: Philosopher and Christian chapter xxxv.— *the Christians condemn and detest all cruelty.*

Contemplative prayer.

"But when ye pray, use not vain repetitions, as the heathen do: for they think that they shall be heard for their much speaking." Matthew 6: 7

EK-KLĀ-SĒ'-Ä - Membership

Creeping into the ek-klā-sē'-ä is this idea from Satan's mind that we must empty our minds by repeating phrases so we can clearly hear God's voice. Then sit quietly and wait to hear and feel the presence of God. There is no such practice in the early church neither should there be today. The practice is just like the practice of meditation in eastern religions and not valid for Christians.

> It is not possible to name the number of the gifts which the Church, [scattered] throughout the whole world, has received from God, in the name of Jesus Christ, who was crucified under Pontius Pilate, and which she exerts day by day for the benefit of the Gentiles, neither practicing deception upon any, nor taking any reward from them[on account of such miraculous interpositions]. For as she has received freely from God, freely also does she minister [to others]. **Nor does she perform anything by means of angelic invocations, or by incantations,or by any other wicked curious art; but, directing her prayers to the Lord, who made all things**, in a pure, sincere, and straightforward spirit, and calling upon the name of our Lord Jesus Christ, she has been accustomed to work miracles for the advantage of mankind,and not to lead them into error. *Irenaeus, AD 178 Against Heresies*
>
> Moreover, it is not the part of a divine spirit to drive the prophetess into such a state of ecstasy and madness that she loses control of herself. *Origen AD 248 Against Celsus.*

The are many in times in Pentecostal and Charismatic services where the person begins to apparently loose control. This is **<u>NOT</u>** the Holy Spirit. And yet this behavior was manifested in the second century. It comes from one of two places, either the person has yielded themselves to demonic powers or it is a show to draw attention to themselves. In either case the leadership must take decisive action. Driving out the demons oppressing the person or rebuke them and bring them back to sanity. One fruit of the Holy Spirit is self-control therefore, to be out of control is not the Holy Spirit.

Other distractions of the Ek-klā-sē'-ä

The enemy of the church finds many ways to make a fellowship ineffective. Should the ek-klā-sē'-ä own property? There is no clear direction from the New Testament. I do not say that fellowships should not have buildings only that the buildings should not have the fellowship. Buildings drain money that could better be used for feeding the poor and the widows and evangelism for building that sit empty 75% of the time. Today these buildings are used for purposes that do not directly build up the body. I have seen fellowships made ineffective by building programs. The focus shifts from seeking the will of God, learning and worship to generating money for the new building. I observed more than once fellowships that went from seeking and serving to becoming introverted and self-centered. These fellowships were never the same. Something changes when a fellowship gets a building. All of the trappings of the traditional church come flooding in.

There was a sweet older lady full of the Holy Spirit very helpful and loving. We were meeting in an old warehouse at the time. When the fellowship decided to build a building, there was a sudden shift in her. Where before she would hand out scripture bookmarks she would now talk about nothing but choir robes and things we must have that traditional churches have in their building. The table at the front became a Holy table and children were rebuked for playing near it because it was "holy".

Chuck Missler tells of an incident that happen in a "church building" a woman came running up to the pastor exasperated and said "Pastor the children are chewing gum in the sanctuary", to which the pastor aptly replied "No, the sanctuaries are chewing gum".

Please keep in mind that when the Messiah said "it is finished" that the curtain that separated the Holy of Holies was rent from top to bottom. This gave us direct access to the throne through Yeshua Ha Meschiach. Yeshua fulfilled all of the types and shadows of the Old Testament sacrifices. There is no longer a need for daily or yearly sacrifices. Yeshua's sacrifice was enough for all times. Please do not think I am saying that we should not have reverence for the Lord. We should have more reverence for the Lord but not for buildings and furniture.

> *Jesus, when he had cried again with a loud voice, yielded up the ghost. And, behold, the veil of the temple was rent in twain from the top to the bottom; and the earth did quake, and the rocks rent;*
> Matthew 27:50-51 (KJV)

We now have direct access to the Father through our Messiah.

> *For through him we both have access by one Spirit unto the Father.*
> Eph 2:18 (KJV)

> *And every priest standeth daily ministering and offering oftentimes the same sacrifices, which can never take away sins: But this man, after he had offered one sacrifice for sins for ever, sat down on the right hand of God; From henceforth expecting till his enemies be made his footstool. For by one offering he hath perfected for ever them that are sanctified. Whereof the Holy Ghost also is a witness to us: for after that he had said before, This is the covenant that I will make with them after those days, saith the Lord, I will put my laws into their hearts, and in their minds will I write them; And their sins and iniquities will I remember no more. Now where remission of these is, there is no more offering for sin. Having therefore, brethren, boldness to enter into the holiest by the blood of Jesus, By a new and living way, which he hath consecrated for us, through the veil, that is to say, his flesh; And having an high priest over the house of God; Let us draw near with a true heart in full assurance of faith, having our hearts sprinkled from an evil conscience, and our bodies washed with pure water.*
> Heb 10:11-22 (KJV)

Your Body is the temple of the Holy Spirit

> *Know ye not that ye are the temple of God, and that the Spirit of God dwelleth in you? If any man defile the temple of God, him shall God destroy; for the temple of God is holy, which temple ye are.*
> 1 Corinthians 3:16-17 (KJV)

> *What? know ye not that your body is the temple of the Holy Ghost which is in you, which ye have of God, and ye are not your own? For*

> ye are bought with a price: therefore glorify God in your body, and in your spirit, which are God's. 1 Corinthians 6:19-20 (KJV)

Together both Jews and Gentiles are together as the body of Christ are characterized as the temple

> Christianity is not a spectator sport

> For he is our peace, who hath made both one, and hath broken down the middle wall of partition between us; Having abolished in his flesh the enmity, even the law of commandments contained in ordinances; for to make in himself of twain one new man, so making peace; And that he might reconcile both unto God in one body by the cross, having slain the enmity thereby: And came and preached peace to you which were afar off, and to them that were nigh. For through him we both have access by one Spirit unto the Father. Now therefore ye are no more strangers and foreigners, but fellowcitizens with the saints, and of the household of God; And are built upon the foundation of the apostles and prophets, Jesus Christ himself being the chief corner stone; In whom all the building fitly framed together groweth unto an holy temple in the Lord: In whom ye also are builded together for an habitation of God through the Spirit. Ephesians 2:14-22 (KJV)

We must remember that the body of Christ is not a building. It is when we forget this that the building becomes sacred and not the people in it. When the organism becomes an organization, the fellowship is on its way toward death and its usefulness become void.

The Birth of the ekklāsē'ä.

In Acts 2 with the great outpouring of the Spirit, the Word tells us that about 3,000 souls were added to them. It makes no mention of these 3,000 becoming members of a church (ekklāsē'ä). They had fellowship and ate meals together and if any had a need they would share with each other as members of the same family. They had fellowship which comes from the Greek word κοινωνία koinōnia. Thayer's Definition[3]: is fellowship, association, community, communion, joint participation.

EK-KLĀ-SĒ'-Ä - Membership

> Now when they heard this, they were pricked in their heart, and said unto Peter and to the rest of the apostles, Men and brethren, what shall we do? Then Peter said unto them, Repent, and be baptized every one of you in the name of Jesus Christ for the remission of sins, and ye shall receive the gift of the Holy Ghost. For the promise is unto you, and to your children, and to all that are afar off, even as many as the Lord our God shall call. And with many other words did he testify and exhort, saying, Save yourselves from this untoward* generation. Then they that gladly received his word were baptized: and the same day there were added unto them about three thousand souls. And they continued stedfastly in the apostles' doctrine and fellowship, and in breaking of bread, and in prayers. And fear came upon every soul: and many wonders and signs were done by the apostles. And all that believed were together, and had all things common; And sold their possessions and goods, and parted them to all men, as every man had need. And they, continuing daily with one accord in the temple, and breaking bread from house to house, did eat their meat with gladness and singleness of heart, Praising God, and having favour with all the people. And the Lord added to the church daily such as should be saved. Acts 2:37-47

* untoward: σκολιός skol-ee-os' - means crooked, curved. It is where we get our word Scoliosis or curvature of the spine.

There are many things I wished they would have expounded on in the text but we are not given a lot of detail in this section about all that happened.

The Church Has Christ as the Only Head

> And hath put all things under his feet, and gave him to be the head over all things to the church [ekklāsē'ä], Which is his body, the fullness of him that filleth all in all. Ephesians 1:22-23 (KJV)

> Wives, submit yourselves unto your own husbands, as unto the Lord. For the husband is the head of the wife, even as Christ is the head of the church [ekklāsē'ä]: and he is the saviour of the body. Therefore as the church is subject unto Christ, so let the wives be to their own husbands in every thing. Ephesians 5:22-24 (KJV)

EK-KLĀ-SĒ'-Ä - Membership

> *And he is the head of the body, the church [ekklāsē'ä]: who is the beginning, the firstborn from the dead; that in all things he might have the preeminence. Colossians 1:18*

There is one head of the ek-klā-sē'-ä ; Jesus Christ. The fact that we have many denominational factions is an indication of how successful Satan has been in dividing us. To me a fully functioning assembly [ekklāsē'ä] is where each one has a place in the body. No one is a passive spectator.

The fact that we have professionally paid "clergy" is a deterrent for the average believer. Why? because it removes the believer's responsibility to know and understand the Word and the Lord for himself or herself. The normal Christian life for most believers is going and hearing a message one or in some cases three times a week. Then living the rest of the time for themselves.

I believe that growth of the members happens in small groups of people because of the accountability and the ability for all to participate and contribute to the conversation. It would serve the enemy well if we were ignorant of the scriptures and void of a "personal" relationship with Yeshua. This is clearly seen today that many Christians are accepting deviant lifestyles as acceptable; homosexuality, abortion, adultery, fornication, lying and the list goes on. I blame the current church structure which by its vary nature keeps people in ignorance. And until brave men like Tyndale and many and others who dared to make the scriptures available to the common man, the Catholic church was able to keep the masses under their control by their ignorance. If someone tells you that only they can interpret the Word, run, do not walk to the nearest exit. You are personally responsible to know the Word. Today there is no excuse.

In appendix A have a short list of resources which can help you learn and understand the Word.

I prefer teaching in small groups because people are not afraid to ask questions. Many times these questions cause me to dig a little deeper to find the truth of the Word. The question that comes to mind, "are my beliefs based on the Word or on tradition?". Are they based on bias?

Tough questions are necessary because it shakes our knowledge base and causes us to seek God's wisdom for the answer. I rarely will try to answer a difficult question on the fly. The question in my mind: is it possible that my understanding has come from the traditions of man rather than the Word of God? It is so easy to get caught up in faulty doctrine because we have heard it taught so often. It is critical that we stop and take time to evaluate what we believe. Passing on the teaching of a denomination or man without checking on it yourself is very dangerous and leads to false doctrine. I will repeat myself "Do not believe anything I say without checking it out yourself".

All men are capable of passing on bias as truth. The exception is the Word of God, the 66 books, we can trust in its original language. Translations are subject to the translator. I suggest that you **_NEVER_** read paraphrased bibles. These are far more likely to pass on the bias and beliefs of the paraphraser than even translations. Additionally, we must know that the Bible is a Jewish book and in order to properly interpret the meaning we must first of all understand the times and the culture in which they were written. Many false doctrines get started because there is no understanding of the Hebrew roots of the Word.

If the body is not fully operational having all of our parts working together we can not function properly. Just as your physical body would not function as it was created if all parts are not operational. Paul makes this point.

> *For as the body is one, and hath many members, and all the members of that one body, being many, are one body: so also is Christ. For by one Spirit are we all baptized into one body, whether we be Jews or Gentiles, whether we be bond or free; and have been all made to drink into one Spirit. For the body is not one member, but many. If the foot shall say, Because I am not the hand, I am not of the body; is it therefore not of the body? And if the ear shall say, Because I am not the eye, I am not of the body; is it therefore not of the body? If the whole body were an eye, where were the hearing? If the whole were hearing, where were the smelling? But now hath God set the members every one of them in the body, as it hath pleased*

EK-KLĀ-SĒ'-Ä - Membership

him. And if they were all one member, where were the body? But now are they many members, yet but one body. And the eye cannot say unto the hand, I have no need of thee: nor again the head to the feet, I have no need of you. Nay, much more those members of the body, which seem to be more feeble, are necessary: And those members of the body, which we think to be less honourable, upon these we bestow more abundant honour; and our uncomely parts have more abundant comeliness. For our comely parts have no need: but God hath tempered the body together, having given more abundant honour to that part which lacked: That there should be no schism in the body; but that the members should have the same care one for another. And whether one member suffer, all the members suffer with it; or one member be honoured, all the members rejoice with it. 1 Cor 12:12-26 (KJV)

For even as the body is one and has many members, and all the members of the body being many, are one body, thus also is the Christ, for indeed by means of one Spirit we all were placed into one body, whether Jews or Gentiles, whether slaves or free men. And we all were imbued (saturated) with one Spirit.
1 Corinthians 12:12-30

My main complaint against modern church structure is that generally speaking one man or some small number of people do everything. In the ek-klā-sē'-ä everyone should be active in some capacity. The failure to do so makes a very lopsided and ineffective organism. Christianity is not a spectator sport.

Why is there a requirement in denominational churches to pledge allegiance to an organization in the form of church membership? If you are a believer you are already a part of the body of Christ. And I challenge you to find in the Word where there is a requirement for membership in a local assembly.

And as for you, you are Christ's body and members individually.
1 Corinthians 12:27

Or is it in fact a strategy to keep members loyal to a particular set of beliefs or to track tithes made by the member? I see no place in scripture where allegiances are made to a local assembly or a denomination. I am not saying that organizations are inherently bad, but if they divide the body it is an indication of something is wrong. Paul shows us that in the early church there was indication of these types of divisions

> *Now I beseech you, brethren, by the name of our Lord Jesus Christ, that ye all speak the same thing, and that there be no divisions among you; but that ye be perfectly joined together in the same mind and in the same judgment. For it hath been declared unto me of you, my brethren, by them which are of the house of Chloe, that there are contentions among you. Now this I say, that every one of you saith, I am of Paul; and I of Apollos; and I of Cephas; and I of Christ. Is Christ divided? was Paul crucified for you? or were ye baptized in the name of Paul?*
> 1 Corinthians 1:10-13 (KJV)

We have a very similar situation today as it was in Paul's day except the names have changed. Now it is I am of Luther or I am of Wesley the list could go on. This should not be but it is the reality of our day. We are simply followers of Yeshua Ha Meschiach, Jesus the Messiah.

James indicates that wherever you see jealousy and contentiousness you will find restlessness and instability and every base deed.

> *Who is a wise man and endued with knowledge among you? let him shew out of a good conversation his works with meekness of wisdom. But if ye have bitter envying and strife in your hearts, glory not, and lie not against the truth. This wisdom descendeth not from above, but is earthly, sensual, devilish. For where envying and strife is, there is confusion and every evil work. But the wisdom that is from above is first pure, then peaceable, gentle, and easy to be intreated, full of mercy and good fruits, without partiality, and without hypocrisy. And the fruit of righteousness is sown in peace of them that make peace. James 3:13-18 (KJV)*

In today's mega-church era the speaker (I call them speakers because they cannot shepherd the flock by themselves) speaks at each service. Where is the discipleship, the accountability in these churches today? The focus becomes one of listening to a sermon for an hour (sometimes via a video link and sometimes less than 30 minutes) and then going home and living a self-focused life having fulfilled the obligation of attendance. In some mega churches the messages seem to be all about what God will do for you. This makes for great attendance but what does it do to prepare the flock? Most of these messages are based loosely on the Word but built around the pop psychology of the day. This does not equip the saints to do the work of the ministry.

This is "feel good" Christianity and of very little value. In the coming days if you are a true believer, it will be essential that you are equipped and knowledgeable about the ways of the enemy. Otherwise, you will be destroyed.

I can tell you first hand that this "Successful Living" teaching works. For years while following these teachings of success in life, I prospered. Each year I was promoted and made more and more money. To the point where I had a two story five bedroom house, an office, with a large pool in the back yard and two German cars. It seemed we had arrived. However, with all of that blessing, I became very cold towards the Lord. Why? Because the focus of my life became "ME". This is known in biblical terms as lukewarm. Having your foot in both camps; the world's and the Lord's. You have heard the old saying that it is not wrong to have things as long as things don't have you. And that it is the LOVE of money that is at the root of all evil. We must ask ourselves if Yeshua (Jesus) is Lord. Are we earth dwellers or sojourners on this earth?

In the end we lost it all. I count that as a blessing. Because the Word tells us "whom the Lord loves he corrects". If you find yourself in a place where you secretly know you are doing wrong (this comes by looking into the mirror of the Word) and the Lord does not correct you... Beware, check your relationship the Lord.

> *"For where your treasure is, there will your heart be also".*
> *Matthew 6:21.*
>
> *And ye have forgotten the exhortation which speaketh unto you as unto children, My son, despise not thou the chastening of the Lord, nor faint when thou art rebuked of him: For whom the Lord*

loveth he chasteneth, and scourgeth every son whom he receiveth. If ye endure chastening, God dealeth with you as with sons; for what son is he whom the father chasteneth not? **But if ye be without chastisement, whereof all are partakers, then are ye bastards, and not sons.** *Furthermore we have had fathers of our flesh which corrected us, and we gave them reverence: shall we not much rather be in subjection unto the Father of spirits, and live?* Hebrews 12:5-9 (KJV)

The Emergent Church

The Emergent Church is very loosely defined. There is no organized denomination called the Emergent Church. However, there are several people who make up this new way of thinking which is to make their services acceptable to all, believing and unbelieving. I believe that the initial stages of this way of thinking came about because the "church" was losing members at an alarming rate. Therefore in order to retain membership a new way of attracting and retaining members was needed.

There is a group who turned to a secular management guru for advice on how to grow their congregations. Peter Drucker, The Father of Management Theory is quite well known and respected in business circles. He guided these churches and taught them how to grow mega churches and his theories work. These followers of Peter Drucker have some of the largest congregations in the world. But at what expense? It reminds me of King Asa, of whom we spoke of in the introduction, rather than seeking the Lord for guidance he called upon a pagan king to help him, remember the result?

Rather than a call to Godly living and repentance and a return to the preaching of the word, an experience was sought which would "entertain" the seeker. This is also known as "seeker friendly" churches. By making the service palatable to even the most carnal, they retain and gain membership. However discipleship, service, holy living and the Word of God are sacrificed for having a growing congregation.

I have heard one prominent member of this movement indicate that even homosexuality is acceptable. We have already pointed out that the Bible is very clear as well as the very early church fathers on this in many passages, homosexuality is an abomination.

This brings me to the next question which is what is the purpose of the ekklāsēä? Is it to get as many people together as we can, to have mega churches so we can do good works and help the people of the world and to bring peace? A great deception in this day is that Christianity is all about doing good works. We don't do good works to be Christian, good works are a result of **being** Christian. Because we are sojourners on this earth our hope is in the next age not this one. Many will find at judgment day that it was not good works that saved them. Christianity is not about religion and good works it is about a personal born again relationship with our Lord Yeshua.

> *Not every one that saith unto me, Lord, Lord, shall enter into the kingdom of heaven; but he that doeth the will of my Father which is in heaven. Many will say to me in that day, Lord, Lord, have we not prophesied in thy name? and in thy name have cast out devils? and in thy name done many wonderful works? And then will I profess unto them, I never knew you: depart from me, ye that work iniquity. Matt 7:21-23 (KJV)*

The kingdom will not be established until the second coming and the beginning of the 1000 year reign of Yeshua on Earth.

Membership in the ek-klā-sē'-ä is fulfilled by attendance. Membership in the body of Christ can only be obtained by being born again.

1 *Word Studies from the Greek New Testament* - Kenneth S. Wuest - William B. Eerdmans Publishing Company.
2 *Alford's Greek Testament* - Henry A. Alford - Out of Print?
3 *Thayer's Greek-English Lexicon of the New Testament:* by Joseph Thayer Publisher: Baker Academic

Chapter XXXVII.—**Christ is our leader, and we His Soldiers.**

Let us then, men and brethren, with all energy act the part of soldiers, in accordance with His holy commandments. Let us consider those who serve under our generals, with what order, obedience, and submissiveness they perform the things which are commanded them. All are not prefects, nor commanders of a thousand, nor of a hundred, nor of fifty,
nor the like, but each one in his own rank performs the things commanded by the king and the generals. The great cannot subsist without the small, nor the small without the great. There is a kind of mixture in all things, and thence arises mutual advantage. Let us take our body for an example. The head is nothing without the feet, and the feet are nothing without the head; yea, the very smallest members of our body are necessary and useful to the whole body. But all work harmoniously together, and are under one common rule for the preservation of the whole body.

Clement of Rome - *The First Epistle of Clement to the Corinthians*

What is the Purpose of The ekklāsē'ä

EK-KLĀ-SĒ'-Ä - Purpose

Have you ever stopped and wondered, what is the purpose of a "church"? I don't think that many have considered it. The church of today is not an example of the original intent and purpose of the gathering. For so many decades we have had structures which were designed by men to govern their churches. The most common form of church government is the "hierarchical". The hierarchical form has several layers of what I will call for lack of a better term managers commonly known as clergy. It wasn't until the fourth century that this clergy versus laity became the norm. It was during this time that Constantine put in leadership men who wre not called by the Lord and those who by one means or another bought their position. It is no wonder that the church took a turn from God to paganism. This was the beginning of the dark ages where people were kept from knowing the living God but had to get their relationship from non-Christian clergy! Nowhere in scripture do we see this structure. The scriptures teach that we are all a kingdom of priests unto God.

> *Rev 1:6 and has made us a kingdom, priests for his God and Father, be glory and power forever and ever! Amen. (International Standard Bible)*

> *And hath made us kings and priests unto God and his Father; to him be glory and dominion for ever and ever. Amen.*
> *Rev 1:6 (KJV)*

The King James version does not clearly interpret the verse because the original Greek says we are a kingdom of priests not kings and priests. The point is that we are all priests unto God. There is no biblical concept of clergy and laity. Whatever the intent was, this structure divides people into "spiritual" and "non-spiritual" by its design.

We will discover in the chapter on leadership that there are only two offices in the New Testament church; the Bishop and the Deacon. The functions of the "four fold ministries" (I will explain why four in the chapter on leadership) specifically provided by the Lord to equip the saints (all of us) to do the work of the ministry. We are all called into full time ministry! The problem is that we have forgotten that fact. We have paid professionals that do that for us. This should never be, we are called-out ones meaning that we are no longer our own. Yeshua said you shall be witnesses.

But ye shall receive power, after that the Holy Ghost is come upon you: and ye shall be witnesses unto me both in Jerusalem, and in all Judaea, and in Samaria, and unto the uttermost part of the earth. Acts 1:8

During the Old Testament period there was a select group, the Levites, which were set a side to do the work of ministry. When Yeshua said it was finished there was no longer a need for sacrifices since he fulfilled all of the law. We are now all priests unto God. We should all do the work of the priest in serving the Lord. We will discuss the types and shadows found in the tabernacle, the priesthood and the offerings in another book.

Discipleship

Go ye therefore, and teach all nations, baptizing them in the name of the Father, and of the Son, and of the Holy Ghost: Teaching them to observe all things whatsoever I have commanded you: and, lo, I am with you alway, even unto the end of the world. Amen. Matthew 28:19-20 (KJV)

> Teach is Strong's G3100. μαθητεύω mathēteúō; to be a disciple or follower of another's doctrine (Matthew. 27:57); to make a disciple (Matthew. 28:19; Acts 14:21); to instruct (Matt. 13:52) with the purpose of making a disciple. - Zodhiates Complete Word Dictionary[1]

The Question we must ask: "is the church creating disciples or members"? It is easy enough to get members, ask any mega church, they will tell you how it is done. But to create disciples takes a much different approach and commitment. I recommend *The Cost of Discipleship* a book by Dietrich Bonhoeffer. Bonhoeffer's story is a very interesting one. He talks about "cheap grace" verses "costly grace"

> "costly grace confronts us as a gracious call to follow Jesus, it comes as a word of forgiveness to the broken spirit and the contrite heart. It is costly because it compels a man to submit to the yoke of Christ and follow him; it is grace because Jesus says: "My yoke is easy and my burden is light."

The church must be in the habit of discipling not only conversions and membership. That takes a much larger commitment, one I am afraid the churches of today have abandoned in favor of church growth and good works. I believe that this is why believers are leaving. The churches are failing to bring people into a fully committed life of love for the Lord and abandonment of the world. Please think about what John said:

> *Love not the world, neither the things that are in the world. If any man love the world, the love of the Father is not in him. For all that is in the world, the lust of the flesh, and the lust of the eyes, and the pride of life, is not of the Father, but is of the world. And the world passeth away, and the lust thereof: but he that doeth the will of God abideth for ever. 1 John 2:15-17 (KJV)*

In many of today's churches they teach how to be successful in today's world. How God will bless you now. He does bless us now but not because we pursue it. There is greater joy in serving and living for the Lord and others than you will ever get from the temporal things of this life.

Equipping the saints

Jon Nielson who is the college pastor at College Church in Wheaton, Illinois writes in an article called *3 Common Traits of Youth Who Don't Leave the Church* explains why youth don't leave the church. The first reason is they have a true born-again experience, two they have been equipped not entertained, and three their parents actually lived and taught them the gospel while growing up. I encourage you to read his full article at: *http://www.faithit.com/3-common-traits-of-youth-who-dont-leave-the-church/?c=fbo*

Obviously if the person is not born-again they can never stand up to the wiles of the devil or to peer pressure. The third reason is also obvious. Being taught the word growing up in a substantial way along with living a genuine life style that is not hypocritical, makes it less likely for a youth to fall away when the pressure comes. Many Christian denounce their faith in college because they were never equipped to a make a stand against the influence of ungodly peers and the humanistic professors who make it their business to ridicule the Bible and Christian beliefs. If a person is not thoroughly trained in the Word and by a good example, they will fall when the pressure comes. They should be equipped to lead someone to the Lord and teach the Word. But I want to focus on his number two reason.

The focus on entertainment rather than discipleship applies not only to young people but to people of all ages. He is correct, most churches find it necessary to entertain their congregations to keep them coming back. This is the exact opposite of what the church should do. It is true that some will come just for the entertainment and food. But this is at the expense of those who are truly wanting to serve God. I am not saying that having some entertainment is bad, but if it takes the place of learning and discipleship the result will be disastrous.

I believe that the assembly is not the only place for evangelism. Jesus told his disciples to go into the highways and byways to make disciples and teach them to observe his commands.

The nature of the standard church structure ends up operating like this: bring your friends to church or the youth group so the pastor, evangelist or youth leader can lead them to salvation. The structure takes the responsibility out of the hands of the believer and puts it on a small group or one "leader". We all as a kingdom of priests are called to do the work of the ministry.

> *And it is he who gifted some to be apostles, others to be prophets, others to be evangelists, and still others to be pastors and teachers, to* ***equip the saints, to do the work of ministry****, and to build up the body of the Messiah*
> Ephesians 4:11-12 (International Standard Bible)

Notice that the saints (all of us who are called by His name) are to do the work of the ministry. The current structure puts the burden on leaders to do the work, you get them to church and they will do the rest. This causes the fellowships to be weak and ineffective because the people are not equipped. (All parts of the body must be built up!) It takes the responsibility from the believer and puts it on the "clergy". I will emphasize that we are told to go make disciples, teaching them to follow the commandments of the Lord.

> *Therefore, as you go, disciple people in all nations, baptizing them in the name of the Father, and the Son, and the Holy Spirit, teaching them to obey everything that I've commanded you. And remember, I am with you each and every day until the end of the age."* Matthew 28:19,20 (International Standard Bible)

The church will continue to lose true Christians who feel that something is missing in their life by attending these watered down fellowships. In recent years many Christians have been leaving the "church". Have they given up on the Lord? I don't believe they have but the "church" is not fulfilling its purpose. The services have become predictable and boring. The response of organizations have been to make the service more enjoyable by exciting music and speeches that thrill the listener. "Come see what God can do for you" seems to be the call of the day. The music is emotionally stirring but five minutes after leaving the "service" that emotion disappears. The question is: after attending the gathering were you convicted, did you learn anything, were you equipped to deal with the world and live a Godly life?

This brings to mind what Paul said to the Colossians:

> *See to it that no one enslaves you through philosophy and empty deceit according to human tradition, according to the basic principles of the world, and not according to the Messiah,*
> Colossians 2:8 International Standard Bible[2]

It is curious that the TV evangelists and traveling circuit preachers/teachers will say "seed into my ministry and God will bless you" or "buy my teachings", while living in luxury and amassing fortunes. While the early church had "all things in common" these "ministers" will take a widows last dime and give nothing in return except some trinket or teaching. One man in particular had two mansions and a yacht. Others have private jets and live the life of a rock star. This is certainly **_NOT_** they way of the New Testament Church.

Paul gives us a clue as to what it truly means to serve the Lord with gladness in 2 Corinthians 11. If these men and women of faith had to live the way Paul did, do you think they would continue, or would they quit at the first sign of persecution? For the most part these people are thieves robbing God's people for their own gain.

It reminds me of the story Yeshua told about the rich man and the beggar. "While you were on earth you had everything and the beggar had nothing. Now you have what you deserve. Is it possible that these wealthy men and women of faith that have it all here will not have their reward there? Only God knows for sure.

Are they ministers of Christ? (I speak as a fool) I am more; in labours more abundant, in stripes above measure, in prisons more frequent, in deaths oft. Of the Jews five times received I forty stripes save one. Thrice was I beaten with rods, once was I stoned, thrice I suffered shipwreck, a night and a day I have been in the deep; In journeyings often, in perils of waters, in perils of robbers, in perils by mine own countrymen, in perils by the heathen, in perils in the city, in perils in the wilderness, in perils in the sea, in perils among false brethren; In weariness and painfulness, in watchings often, in hunger and thirst, in fastings often, in cold and nakedness. Beside those things that are without, that which cometh upon me daily, the care of all the churches. 2 Corinthians 11:23-28 (KJV)

Please do not think I am saying that God's people should never have nice things. But to fleece the poor and needy who are looking to these charlatans to have the answer from God is shameful. But no one wants to hear about the downside of being a Christian. The prosperity gospel works because the enemy wants us to get our minds off of Him and on to the goods we can acquire. We are not in this world to store up treasures here on earth, this is not biblical.

> *But thou hast fully known my doctrine, manner of life, purpose, faith, longsuffering, charity, patience, Persecutions, afflictions, which came unto me at Antioch, at Iconium, at Lystra; what persecutions I endured: but out of them all the Lord delivered me. Yea, and* **all that will live godly in Christ Jesus shall suffer persecution.** *2 Timothy 3:10-12 (KJV)*

We were associated with a group in Minnesota who had a camp. Each summer we would drive to northern Minnesota to attend one of the yearly camps. Everything was done on an offering basis. There was no set charge for the camp just give what you can. Even the books and tapes could be obtained on a donation basis. The only requirement was that you would have some duty to perform while you were there; cleaning, cooking, washing dishes among other things. Today we see these traveling speakers make themselves wealthy by selling books and CDs. Would they come and rent these enormous stadiums and hotels if they were not going to pull in a lot of money? How does this compare to the apostles who traveled mostly on foot or by boat?

> *For in what respect were you put to a disadvantage in comparison with the rest of the churches, unless [it was for the fact] that I myself* **did not burden you [with my financial support]?** *Pardon me [for*

*doing you] this injustice! Now for the third time I am ready to come to [visit] you. And **I will not burden you [financially], for it is not your [money] that I want but you**; for children are not duty bound to lay up store for their parents, but parents for their children. But I will most gladly spend [myself] and be utterly spent for your souls. If I love you exceedingly, am I to be loved [by you] the less? But though granting that **I did not burden you [with my support**, some say that] I was crafty [and that] I cheated and got the better of you with my trickery. Did I [then] take advantage of you or make any money out of you through any of those [messengers] whom I sent to you? [Actually] I urged Titus [to go], and I sent the brother with [him]. **Did Titus overreach or take advantage of you** [in anything]? Did he and I not act in the same spirit ? Did we not [take the] same steps? Have you been supposing [all this time] that we have been defending ourselves and apologizing to you ? [It is] in the sight and the [very] presence of God [and as one] in Christ (the Messiah) that we have been speaking, dearly beloved, and all in order to build you up [spiritually]. 2 Corinthians 12:13-19 Amplified³*

These TV and traveling preachers are fond of quoting 1 Timothy 5:18:

Let the elders that rule well be counted worthy of double honour, especially they who labour in the word and doctrine. For the scripture saith, Thou shalt not muzzle the ox that treadeth out the corn. And, The labourer is worthy of his reward.
1 Timothy 5:17-18 (KJV)

I agree that you should not muzzle the ox. But these people are not elders in a local body. Just where do these TV evangelists and traveling preachers fit in the body at large? And is what they are doing biblical and right? Should the flock be fed by the local leadership and by visiting dignitaries, those who are called to be apostles, prophets and teachers and submitted to the local fellowships?   In many ways these people are usurping the authority of the local leadership. Are they being held accountable for what they say and teach? Can they be held accountable? Does the local leadership know what the flock is being taught?

EK-KLĀ-SĒ'-Ä - Purpose

Like the Internet people who can say anything they want, which does not have to be true. It is no wonder that the body is confused there are so many mixed messages being tossed around these days. Back in 1948, the Lord spoke to a man and told him that the enemy was about to unleash a very powerful weapon. That or near that year television became a reality as well as the beginnings of the Internet. It has been proved to be true on both accounts.

Just compensation and over compensation are two different things. Getting wealthy from preaching the Word to me is tantamount to what Simon Magus did in trying to buy the ability to pray for people so they could receive the Holy Spirit (see Acts 8:14-25). It does not seem right to prosper on the backs of the people. It is my intent to always offer what I have to the Lord without a price tag. The Lord will supply all my needs according to his riches. I hope that I can always say like Paul:

> *Not that I speak in respect of want: for I have learned, in whatsoever state I am, therewith to be content. I know both how to be abased, and I know how to abound: everywhere and in all things I am instructed both to be full and to be hungry, both to abound and to suffer need. I can do all things through Christ which strengtheneth me. Phillipians 4:11-13 (KJV)*

In 2 Corinthians 8, Paul lays out a very interesting truth about finances. Quoting from Exodus 16:18 concerning the gathering of the daily manna in the wilderness: "**He that had gathered much had nothing over; and he that had gathered little had no lack.**". If one group has been abundantly blessed and there is another group who is currently under financial duress, the one should ease the burden of the other. God's way of finance is that everyone should have what they need but not to excess. Do you think that these famous preachers give of their abundance to others that are struggling; or do we find them living a life of excess and luxury?

> *I speak not by commandment, but by occasion of the forwardness of others, and to prove the sincerity of your love. For ye know the grace of our Lord Jesus Christ, that, though he was rich, yet for your sakes he became poor, that ye through his poverty might be rich. And herein I give my advice: for this is expedient for you, who*

> *have begun before, not only to do, but also to be forward a year ago. Now therefore perform the doing of it; that as there was a readiness to will, so there may be a performance also out of that which ye have. For if there be first a willing mind, it is accepted according to that a man hath, and not according to that he hath not. For I mean not that other men be eased, and ye burdened:* **But by an equality, that now at this time your abundance may be a supply for their want, that their abundance also may be a supply for your want**: *that there may be equality: As it is written, He that had gathered much and had nothing over; and he that had gathered little had no lack.* 2 Corinthians 8:8-15 (KJV)

I am not saying we should be communists or socialists, but out of love for the brethren we should be willing to share what we have, not by coercion, but as a cheerful giver unto the Lord.

I was reading Loren Cunningham's book *Daring to Live On the Edge* and read a quote which I thinks sums it up in his chapter on The Question of Affluence.

> "How do you know if you're living too far above (or below) those among whom you are ministering? Ask yourself this question: *Is this (car, house, lifestyle) helping me or hindering me in winning and discipling people for Jesus?*"

He goes on to talk about what Peter said:

> *Feed the flock of God which is among you, taking the oversight thereof, not by constraint, but willingly;* ***not for filthy lucre****, but of a ready mind; Neither as being lords over God's heritage,* ***but being ensamples to the flock.*** *And when the chief Shepherd shall appear, ye shall receive a crown of glory that fadeth not away.*
> 1 Peter 5:2-4 (KJV)

What do you think the world believes about these people when they see the TV preachers and such flaunting their wealth? It is not good I assure you. They see them constantly asking for money, selling trinkets and materials while living far above the average giver. We should be examples for the people we serve.

Don't be fooled by the amounts of money some of these preachers give, it may appear to be a lot but as a percentage of income it may be very low. Remember the widow and her mites:

And Jesus sat over against the treasury, and beheld how the people cast money into the treasury: and many that were rich cast in much. And there came a certain poor widow, and she threw in two mites, which make a farthing. And he called unto him his disciples, and saith unto them, Verily I say unto you, That this poor widow hath cast more in, than all they which have cast into the treasury: For all they did cast in of their abundance; but she of her want did cast in all that she had, even all her living. Mark 12:41-44 (KJV)

Don't forget what Paul told Timothy:

Tell those who are rich in this age not to be arrogant and not to place their confidence in anything as uncertain as riches. Instead, let them place their confidence a in God, who lavishly provides us with everything for our enjoyment. They are to do good, to be rich in good actions, to be generous, and to share. By doing this they store up a treasure for themselves that is a good foundation for the future, so that they can keep their hold on the life that is real.
1 Timothy 6:17-19 (International Standard Version ISV)

I have listened to some of the modern mega church speakers and I find scripture mixed with current day psychology. Can the normal listener distinguish the difference between the pure Word and philosophy of the world? It sounds good, it makes you feel good, but is it the purpose of the Lord? I just read a teaching by a very popular female speaker who was encouraging her readers to "visualize" their outcome. I was horrified! Nowhere in the Word are we told to visualize anything. This is loosely based on modern self-help teaching and in the worst case based on eastern mysticism! I am going to be crass and say that she is being used by Satan to introduce the body to occult practices whether she knows it or not. May she see the error of her way and repent! Mixing the pure Word of God with the secular philosophy of Plato, Aristotle and others is what corrupted some of the early church writers. They were severely rebuked by those who kept the truth of the word and did not stray into false teaching.

Unfortunately, we are seeing more and more of this in our churches. It reminds me of the parable that Jesus told about the tares.

> *Another parable put he forth unto them, saying, The kingdom of heaven is likened unto a man which sowed good seed in his field: But while men slept, his enemy came and sowed tares among the wheat, and went his way. But when the blade was sprung up, and brought forth fruit, then appeared the tares also. So the servants of the householder came and said unto him, Sir, didst not thou sow good seed in thy field? from whence then hath it tares? He said unto them, An enemy hath done this. The servants said unto him, Wilt thou then that we go and gather them up? But he said, Nay; lest while ye gather up the tares, ye root up also the wheat with them. Let both grow together until the harvest: and in the time of harvest I will say to the reapers, Gather ye together first the tares, and bind them in bundles to burn them: but gather the wheat into my barn. Matthew 13:24-30 (KJV)*

The enemy came in and sowed tares and the servants asked if they should go and pull out the tares. They were told no because they might pull up the wheat at the same time. The only difference between wheat and a tare is that wheat has fruit (grain), but you cannot tell that when they are growing, they look the same. This is the situation we have today. How can you tell the false teachers from the true? Because they interleave scripture with philosophy it appears to be right. But what is the fruit of these teachings? It is not to glorify God, but to make the person "feel good" about themselves.

Nowhere in scripture are we told to have good "self-esteem". The prosperity teachers and the hyper-supernaturalists (my word) lead the flock down the wrong path, the path to destruction. We are entering a time of great turmoil we need teaching about relying and trusting completely in the Lord not "you can be rich like me".

If we are in the last days, and I believe we are, things are not going to get better, they are going to get worse. Our days of total religious freedom are ending, you can see it in the news everyday. The birth pangs of persecution are getting more intense. We need to equip our flocks to face what is coming with power from the Holy Spirit; otherwise, the ravenous wolves will tear them to shreds!

Where are the true shepherds? These TV personalities have no responsibility to the people they speak to; they are like foxes that invade the hen house while the shepherds sleep. What started out as evangelical outreach has become a cesspool of false teachers and certainly false prophets.

> Responding to Pat Robertson's comments that Young Earth Creationists are "deaf, dumb and blind," Ken Ham of the Creation Museum accused the CBN host of compromising Scripture and thus serving as "one of the biggest problems we have today in the church."

We must for the sake of the flock get back to a New Testament mind set, and thus the reason for writing this book. It sounds like what Paul told Timothy would happen in the last days.

> *For the time will come when they will not endure sound doctrine; but after their own lusts shall they heap to themselves teachers, having itching ears; 2Timothy 4:3*

At the same time, we see a rise in the acceptance of deviant life styles. All pointing at how ineffective the church has become as it moves away from its purpose. Many organizations have abandoned the leading of the Holy Spirit for rigid structures which guarantee they will remain in control. Go into almost any denomination today and as you enter the service you will be given an agenda (the church bulletin). The document lays out in detail what the service will be that day. Two or three hymns, announcements, a very short sermon followed by another hymn. In evangelical churches there may be an alter call.

Paul in Corinthians gives us insight to what the early church gathering was like as well as some of the mistakes. We will take up the operation of the gifts later, for now, I want to discuss the purpose of the assembly.

> *What, then, does this mean, brothers? When you gather, everyone has a psalm, teaching, revelation, other language, or interpretation.*

EK-KLĀ-SĒ'-Ä - Purpose

Everything must be done for upbuilding.
1Corinthians 14:26 (International Standard Bible)

How is it then, brethren? when ye come together, every one of you hath a psalm, hath a doctrine, hath a tongue, hath a revelation, hath an interpretation. Let all things be done unto edifying. (KJV)

It is obvious that there was no formal "clergy". Paul did not say let the bishops direct the service and only they should speak. Everyone had something to contribute. Because of their enthusiasm there was some confusion in the meeting. Paul was making the point that there should be some order but did not say they should have a structured agenda, only that things should be done in an orderly fashion. He also indicates that each one speaking should be judged.

If any man speak in an unknown tongue, let it be by two, or at the most by three, and that by course; and let one interpret. But if there be no interpreter, let him keep silence in the church; and let him speak to himself, and to God. Let the prophets speak two or three, and let the other judge. If any thing be revealed to another that sitteth by, let the first hold his peace. For ye may all prophesy one by one, that all may learn, and all may be comforted. And the spirits of the prophets are subject to the prophets. For God is not the author of confusion, but of peace, as in all churches of the saints.
1 Corinthians 14:27-33 (KJV)

This disorder is the main reason people decided that they should control the gathering by not allowing the gifts to operate in the assembly. In today's modern church the Holy Spirit is not invited to lead a gathering, that job has been taken over by man in order to avoid a "messy and disruptive" service. The end result of that dictate is a rejection of the gifts altogether. Some will even be so bold as to suggest that the gifts do not exist today. We will discuss why they do exist today when addressing the gifts specifically in the chapter on the operation of the New Testament Church.

The purpose of the ek-klā-sē'-ä is to build up the body of Christ, to equip the saints to do the work of the ministry, to exhort each other, to provoke all to love and good works. The day of being simply a separator is over. In these turbulent times we must be equipped for what is about to come. It

EK-KLĀ-SĒ'-Ä - Purpose

is obvious that the season is changing and we must be ready. The apostasy has already started and some organizations are leading the flock over the cliff to be eaten by the wolves who are ready to devour the apostate church. Wake up and rebuild what remains by heeding the call to return to a New Testament way of living, following the teachings of Yeshua and the Apostles.

> *Having therefore, brethren, boldness to enter into the holiest by the blood of Jesus, By a new and living way, which he hath consecrated for us, through the veil, that is to say, his flesh; And having an high priest over the house of God; Let us draw near with a true heart in full assurance of faith, having our hearts sprinkled from an evil conscience, and our bodies washed with pure water.* **Let us hold fast the profession of our faith without wavering; (for he is faithful that promised;) And let us consider one another to provoke unto love and to good works: Not forsaking the assembling of ourselves together, as the manner of some is; but exhorting one another: and <u>so much the more, as ye see the day approaching.</u>** *Hebrews 10:19-25 (KJV)*

---

1 - *Complete Word Study Dictionary* - Dr. Spiros Zodhiates - AMG Publishers
2 - International Standard Bible - The ISV Foundation Committee on Translation - Davidson Press
3 - Amplified Bible - Zondervan Publishing

DISCIPLESHIP

"When Christ calls a man, he bids him come and die."
 - Dietrich Bonhoeffer, *The Cost of Discipleship*

"When all is said and done, the life of faith is nothing if not an unending struggle of the spirit with every available weapon against the flesh." - Dietrich Bonhoeffer, *The Cost of Discipleship*

"Costly grace is the gospel which must be sought again and again and again, the gift which must be asked for, the door at which a man must knock. Such grace is costly because it calls us to follow, and it is grace because it calls us to follow Jesus Christ. It is costly because it costs a man his life, and it is grace because it gives a man the only true life. It is costly because it condemns sin, and grace because it justifies the sinner. Above all, it is costly because it cost God the life of his Son: 'Ye were bought at a price', and what has cost God much cannot be cheap for us. Above all, it is grace because God did not reckon his Son too dear a price to pay for our life, but delivered him up for us. Costly grace is the Incarnation of God."
- Dietrich Bonhoeffer, *The Cost of Discipleship*

Cheap grace is the preaching of forgiveness without requiring repentance, baptism without church discipline, Communion without confession, absolution without personal confession. Cheap grace is grace without discipleship, grace without the cross, grace without Jesus Christ, living and incarnate.
- Dietrich Bonhoeffer, *The Cost of Discipleship*

The proconsul then urged him, saying, "Swear, and I will release thee; -- reproach Christ."

Polycarp answered, "Eighty and six years have I served him, and he never once wronged me; how then shall I blaspheme my King, Who hath saved me?" At the stake, to which he was only tied, but not nailed as usual, as he assured them he should stand immovable, the flames, on their kindling the fagots, encircled his body, like an arch, without touching him, and the executioner, on seeing this, was ordered to pierce him with a sword when so great a quantity of blood flowed out as extinguished the fire. But his body, at the instigation of the enemies of the Gospel, especially Jews, was ordered to be consumed in the pile, and the request of his friends, who wished to give it Christian burial, rejected. They nevertheless collected his bones and as much of his remains as possible, and caused them to be decently interred.

—Foxe's Book of Martyrs

3

Leadership
of The ekklāsē'ä

Primus Inter Pares

A Latin phrase meaning first among equals. This would apply to Peter in Acts chapter 2 and James in Acts chapter 15. Not one over many, but first among equals! The title would be an honorary title given for various reasons but certainly not one that set up one over the many as the final say. It was Ignatius of Antioch who put forth the idea of one man in charge or mono episcopacy. It appears that he thought that unity could only be accomplished by having one man in charge.

> while **_your bishop presides in the place of God_**, and your presbyters in the place of the assembly of the apostles, along with your deacons, who are most dear to me, and are entrusted with the ministry of Jesus Christ, Let nothing exist among you that may divide you; but be ye united with your bishop, and those that preside over you, as a type and evidence of your immortality.
> *The Epistle of Ignatius to the Magnesians*
> Chapter VI.—*Preserve harmony*

We should never let one person rule for the sake of harmony. Right is right and wrong is wrong. When one person other than the Lord and Holy Spirit have the final say then Satan has an open door to deceive and cause irreparable damage. Every cult has a single leader which everyone must obey without question. No, the head of the church is Yeshua and the elders are his under shepherds. The Didache and Polycarp do not agree that one man should have precedence.

> Therefore, choose for yourselves **_bishops and deacons_** worthy of God, men who are gentle, not lovers of money, dependable, and proven, for they also serve you with the service of prophets and teachers. *Didache* 15:1

> Therefore, it is necessary to keep away from all these things, subjecting yourselves to the **_elders and to the deacons_** as to God and to Christ. *Polycarp to the Philippians 5:3*

In the early church there was equality of leadership. Equality of leadership can only work where the leaders are sold out to the Lord who is the head of the church and follow the leading of the Holy Spirit. When leaders begin to depend on their own ideas, when they focus on themselves filled with self-ambition, when integrity wanes, the fellowship will begin to crumble and eventually split or fail. I think of what John Adams said concerning the Constitution of the United States about its inadequacy when morality is gone. Unfortunately, we have arrived at that period of time in our history as a nation where both morality and true Christianity have all but disappeared. Without a swift and decisive move of the Holy Spirit to revive us, I am afraid we are doomed as a nation.

> But should the people of America once become capable of that deep simulation towards one another, and towards foreign nations, which assumes the language of justice and moderation while it is practicing iniquity and extravagance, and displays in the most captivating manner the charming pictures of candor, frankness, and sincerity, while it is rioting in rapine and insolence, this country will be the most miserable habitation in the world; because we have no government armed with power capable of contending with human passions unbridled by morality and religion. Avarice, ambition, revenge, or gallantry, would break the strongest cords of our Constitution as a whale goes through a net. **Our Constitution was made only for a moral and religious people. It is wholly inadequate to the government of any other**. John Adams - 11 October, 1798

There are only two offices in the New Testament church: Elder and Deacon. The fourfold ministries are functions within the body at large. These exist in the local assembly and world-wide. There are those who will function as an apostle at times and maybe a pastor (shepherd) at other times and an evangelist at others. The so called five fold ministry is a function not an office in the church. In fact there are only four functions not five. Dr. Bob Utley commenting on Ephesians 4:11 says the following:

> "pastors and teachers" The titles "elders" (presbuteroi), "bishops" (episkopoi), and "pastors" (poimenas) all refer to one function and later office (cf. Act_20:17; Act_20:28; and Tit_1:5-7). The term "elder" had an OT

background, while the term "bishop" or "overseer" had a Greek city-state background. The Greek syntax (one conjunction [de] and one article [tous]) links these two titles together as one function, **one gifted person who proclaims and explains the gospel to a local situation.** Dr. Bob Utley[3]

And he gave some, apostles; and some, prophets; and some, evangelists; and some, pastors and teachers; Ephesians 4:11

The Greek is very emphatic, "HE GAVE." It was God himself who put these individuals into their functions. There is never an instant where the fellowship voted on deacons and elders. They were appointed after a thorough check of the their background and much prayer and fasting.

In those early days, all were Spirit-filled men who depended solely on God's Spiritual leadership. These were appointed, not voted on. The apostle under the guidance of the Holy Spirit would confirm and appoint Elders and Deacons. Today our great Church leaders rely more upon human wisdom and trained intellects. They believe that churches should move with the times and the culture and do not strictly adhere to the Word of God.

I know of a "pastor" in a large denomination who denied the very word of God stating that it is mostly nice stories and a guide book on how to act. This is heresy! The modern church of today has become a social club, denying the Word and making a mockery of the true meaning of Christianity. If these so called pastors do not believe in the Word, they cannot believe in the Messiah; if they don't believe in Yeshua what is the point, other than to have a social club where people can come and feel like they are doing good.

These churches do a lot of good works; feeding the poor and visiting the sick in the hospital, but, when it comes to discipleship, repentance and obedience to the Lord it is merely empty words. The question is: are we living a life dedicated to the Lord or a self-focused life of the flesh.

Go ye therefore, and teach all nations, baptizing them in the name of the Father, and of the Son, and of the Holy Ghost: **_Teaching_** *them*

> *to observe all things whatsoever I have commanded you: and, lo, I am with you alway, even unto the end of the world. Amen.*
> *Matt 28:19-20 (KJV) Matthew 28:19*

The word <u>teach</u> here only tells part of the story. The word teach is Strong's G3100 μαθητεύω Matheteuo: to be a disciple of one to follow his precepts and instructions. The New King James[1] correctly uses the phrase "make disciples" the International Standard version[2] uses the phrase "Therefore, as you go, disciple people in all nations". The idea here is not to make converts but to disciple those who accept the Messiah and teach them to observe the commands of Yeshua.

In today's fast food generation, the goal is to see how many people can be brought in and converted. The numbers can be astounding but upon closer examination only a very minute number are ever discipled or taught follow the commands of the Lord.

Derek Prince tells of his early experience with the Billy Graham Organization in England. (First I want you to know that I admire Billy Graham and what he has done). Derek tells of getting twenty people from the crusade for whom he was responsible to follow-up and make sure they were established. He was very diligent in his follow up and yet in his estimation only two ever took root. This is not the fault of Derek Prince or of Billy Graham, there are many reasons why some will walk away. It is said that there is a 92% failure rate in evangelical campaigns where so-called "decisions for Christ" end up not producing lasting fruit. Yeshua gives us a clue in the parable of the sower.

> *Behold, a sower went forth to sow; And when he sowed, some seeds fell by the way side, and the fowls came and devoured them up: Some fell upon stony places, where they had not much earth: and forthwith they sprung up, because they had no deepness of earth: And when the sun was up, they were scorched; and because they had no root, they withered away. And some fell among thorns; and the thorns sprung up, and choked them: But other fell into good ground, and brought forth fruit, some an hundredfold, some sixtyfold, some thirtyfold. Who hath ears to hear, let him hear.*
> *Matt 13:3-9 (KJV)*

This current structure called "church" gives the members a false sense of belonging to the kingdom of the Messiah. I have attended some of these congregations. The words they confess are very sound biblically but judging by the fruit of their congregation they are dead. While it is true that faith without works is dead, it is equally true that works without faith is dead. We are saved by grace through faith, not by good works lest any man boast in the fact that he was saved by his works. The deception of our enemy has lulled these people into a false sense of security believing that church membership, attendance and good works will save them and they can live their lives for themselves. The catch phrase is "God won't reject me I am a good person". But on the day of judgment the question will be. Is your name written in the Lamb's book of life? If you are unsure if your name is written in the Lamb's book of life, I suggest you find out what that means.

I am afraid that the modern denominational church is moving farther away from the Lord. This is confirmed by the push for ecumenicism. Technically, unity is what we would want for the body of Christ but not at the cost of compromising the Word of God to "get along". In America we have been able to co-exist with all religions. You are free to believe what you want, right or wrong.

However, the new religion of Humanism will not accept religion in any form. It is their goal to have a society free of religion. They have a plan and they are working it. You can recognize it almost every day, the relentless attack on Christians and Jews. If we do not push back our religious freedoms will disappear overnight. They have already been eroded. And where our Constitution said that "Congress shall make no Law... Establishing religion or denying the free exercise thereof" has been distorted to the point that the framers would not recognize it.

The new government religion is Humanism. The fact that even speaking about creation in a public school can get you fired tells the story and we could give many other illustrations. At every turn Christians are put down and denied the freedom to speak and to carry bibles to school shows that we are being denied the free exercise of our religion.

It is revealing that Islam, Satanism and other cults are not being persecuted. Even though the teaching of Islam is clearly one that does not

EK-KLĀ-SĒ'-Ä - Leadership

accept anyone not professing allegiance to Allah, in fact, where they rule you convert, pay the tax or die. Yet they are not attacked like Christians and Jews. Islam is strictly against homosexuality but it is only the Christians who are targeted for the so called "hate crimes".

I see a lot of bumper stickers which spell out in symbols coexist. Unfortunately, we see into day's world with the rise of radical Muslims that there is no coexisting. Their goal is the annihilation of everyone who does not convert to Islam. It is irrelevant that there are peaceful Muslims; it is the radicals that are causing mass death across the world in the name of Allah. Paul warns Timothy that in the last days men would have the form of godliness but deny its power; they would ever be learning but not come to the truth.

> Polycarp's letter to Philippi speaks only of "presbyters" (plurality of elders), not one bishop. The idea of a single lead elder is not presented here.
>
> *The Epistle of Polycarp to the Philippians*
>
> Polycarp, and the presbyters with him, to the Church of God sojourning at Philippi: Mercy to you, and peace from God Almighty, and from the Lord Jesus Christ, our Saviour, be multiplied.

This know also, that in the last days perilous times shall come. For men shall be lovers of their own selves, covetous, boasters, proud, blasphemers, disobedient to parents, unthankful, unholy, Without natural affection, trucebreakers, false accusers, incontinent, fierce, despisers of those that are good, Traitors, heady, highminded, lovers of pleasures more than lovers of God; Having a form of godliness, but denying the power thereof: from such turn away. For of this sort are they which creep into houses, and lead captive silly women laden with sins, led away with divers lusts, Ever learning, and never able to come to the knowledge of the truth. Now as Jannes and Jambres withstood Moses, so do these also resist the truth: men of corrupt minds, reprobate concerning the faith. But they shall proceed no further: for their folly shall be manifest unto all men, as theirs also was. 2 Tim 3:1-9 (KJV)

In those early days, the evangelists went forth empowered with God's tools for building new assemblies. Today we send forth men and women trained and schooled in denominational church discipline. In the first century, they had no special educational training of great organizations to support and guide them, but a total dependence on the leading and guidance of the Holy Spirit. We, as the body of Christ, have strayed a very long way from total dependence on the Lord to depending on man and man's wisdom. - Glen Ewing Grace Gospel Church

Appointing Leaders

Clement of Rome, we believe, was a convert of Barnabas. He studied under Peter and was familiar with Paul and John. This does not mean his text should be considered scripture and only used as conformation of scripture and a historical reference. He is mentioned by Paul in Philippians.

> *And I intreat thee also, true yokefellow, help those women which laboured with me in the gospel, with Clement also, and with other my fellowlabourers, whose names are in the book of life. Phillipians 4:3 (KJV)*

In Clement's first epistle to the Corinthians (chapter 42) he tells about the apostles appointing bishops and deacons after their first being proved by the Spirit. Please notice that they did not appoint Pastor or any of the so called five fold ministries.

> The apostles have preached the Gospel to us from the Lord Jesus Christ; Jesus Christ[has done so] from God. Christ therefore was sent forth by God, and the apostles by Christ. Both these appointments, then, were made in an orderly way, according to the will of God. Having therefore received their orders, and being fully assured by the resurrection of our Lord Jesus Christ, and established in the word of God, with full assurance of the Holy Ghost, they went forth proclaiming that the kingdom of God was at hand. **And thus preaching through countries and cities, they appointed the first-fruits [of their labours], having first proved them by the Spirit, to be bishops and**

deacons of those who should afterwards believe. Nor was this any new thing, since indeed, many ages before, it was written concerning bishops and deacons. For thus saith the Scripture in a certain place, "I will appoint their bishops in righteousness, and their deacons in faith." *Clement of Rome Chapter XLII.—The order of ministers in the Church.*

We have already stated that there are only two offices in the New Testament church, The Elder (bishop or overseer) and the Deacon. Within this group are typically found the four functions of Apostle, Prophet, Evangelist, Pastor / Teacher but we have no scriptural evidence that they had to be a Bishop or a Deacon since these were local offices within the ek-klā-sē'-ä and most likely did not travel very often to other fellowships in a leadership capacity.

There should never be just one elder. Elders should have co-authority. We see this co-leadership in Acts chapter 15 at the council of Jerusalem where no one apostle was the final say. In Acts (chapter thirteen) they were sent out in pairs, Barnabas and Paul.

There should never be a lead elder. The New Testament never refers to "the pastor" at the church in... There should never be a single teaching elder who does all of the teaching. Christianity is not a democracy but a theocracy where Christ is the head. It is possible for any of us to be deceived, having plurality of leadership generally eliminates this issue. However, if one man rules and has final authority, the opportunity for error increases dramatically.

Additionally, if one man has a powerful charismatic personality and is the center of attention it will be a large problem for the fellowship if this person falls into sin, dies or decides to leave the fellowship. I have seen this scenario many times in my life and the outcome is exactly what the enemy wants; division, disillusionment and sometimes the collapse of a fellowship altogether. It is essential that no one person be the focus of all activity within a fellowship. Remember, there is only one head of the ek-klā-sē'-ä and that is Yeshua himself. The first turn the early church made was called **<u>mono episcopacy</u>**. We can see this in the writing of Ignatius in *The Epistle of Ignatius to the Philadelphians*.

EK-KLĀ-SĒ'-Ä - Leadership

> Take ye heed, then, to have but one Eucharist. For there is one flesh of our Lord Jesus Christ, and one cup to [show forth] the unity of His blood; one altar; <u>as there is one bishop,</u> along with the presbytery and deacons, my fellow-servants: that so, whatsoever ye do, ye may do it according to [the will of] God. Chapter IV.—*Have but one Eucharist*

This belief of one bishop would eventually grow and fester until we have the Pope declared as the "vicar of Christ" (in place of Christ). The Anti-Christ means "in place of Christ". When anything takes precedence over Yeshua it is anti-Christ. We have already stated that Christ is the head of the church. Anyone who usurps that is anti-Christ. The last days started in the days of the Apostles. We are in a time-out between the 69th and 70th week of Daniel. Therefore, we have been in the last days for quite a while. What we know for sure is that when the Man of Sin goes into the rebuilt temple to the Holy of Holies and declares himself to be God the clock starts counting down the last three and one half years before the second coming of the Messiah.

After Constantine moved the capital of Roman the imperial properties he bequeathed to the Bishop and we have the first Pope, Gregory, the First and Leo the First takes the title Pontificate Maximus. Cyprian put forth the idea that in order for God to be your father, the church must be your mother. This is clearly seen in the following quotes:

> Cyprian to the martyrs and confessors in Christ our Lord and in God the Father, everlasting salvation. gladly rejoice and am thankful, most brave and blessed brethren, at hearing of your faith and virtue, **wherein the Church, our Mother, glories**... that those who are united at once by the bond of confession, and the entertainment of a dungeon, may also be united in the consummation of their virtue and a celestial crown; that you by your joy may dry the tears of **our Mother, the Church...** with God's permission, we begin to be gathered together once more into the **bosom of the Church, our Mother**. Concerning Cyprian Epistle VIII. *To the Martyrs and Confessors.*

I think a good example of equality of leadership can be found in an organization which will remain nameless. The books that I have read about the organization indicates that the leadership will come together and seek God's guidance on an issue. If they all agree then the go ahead. If there is any descent they continue to seek the Lord until they are in unity. We have taken that approach in our family. We seek the Lord if we are all in agreement we go ahead, otherwise, we wait until we are unified in our solution.

If there is one man who has the final say, the potential for problems increases dramatically. I have seen this happen more than once. In most cases, if there would have been co-leadership many of the problems could have been avoided. In one specific case four elders were opposed to what a single man (a pastor) wanted to do. If this "pastor" would have listened to the elders, a church split could have been avoided. This ultimately caused the sheep to scatter and this fellowship went from a growing Spirit filled organism to a dying one. The fellowship never again reached its potential and Satan won again by making the ek-klā-sē'-ä ineffectual in that city.

How did the Apostles greet the ek-klā-sē'-ä when writing to them was it: To the Pastor (or Bishop at...) no, the following are just a few examples:

> *Paul, a servant of Jesus Christ, called to be an apostle, separated unto the gospel of God, (Which he had promised afore by his prophets in the holy scriptures,) Concerning his Son Jesus Christ our Lord, which was made of the seed of David according to the flesh; And declared to be the Son of God with power, according to the spirit of holiness, by the resurrection from the dead: By whom we have received grace and apostleship, for obedience to the faith among all nations, for his name: Among whom are ye also the called of Jesus Christ: <u>To all that be in Rome,</u> beloved of God, called to be saints: Grace to you and peace from God our Father, and the Lord Jesus Christ. Romans 1:1-7 (KJV)*

> *Paul, called to be an apostle of Jesus Christ through the will of God, and Sosthenes our brother, <u>Unto the church of God which is at Corinth</u>, to them that are sanctified in Christ Jesus, called to be saints, with all that in every place call upon the name of Jesus Christ our Lord, both theirs and ours: 1 Cor 1:1-2 (KJV)*

EK-KLĀ-SĒ'-Ä - Leadership

Paul, an apostle of Jesus Christ by the will of God, and Timothy our brother, <u>unto the church of God which is at Corinth</u>, with all the saints which are in all Achaia: Grace be to you and peace from God our Father, and from the Lord Jesus Christ. 2 Cor 1:1-2 (KJV)

Paul, an apostle, (not of men, neither by man, but by Jesus Christ, and God the Father, who raised him from the dead;) And all the brethren which are with me, <u>unto the churches of Galatia</u>: Gal 1:1-2 (KJV)

Paul, an apostle of Jesus Christ by the will of God, <u>to the saints which are at Ephesus</u>, and to the faithful in Christ Jesus: Grace be to you, and peace, from God our Father, and from the Lord Jesus Christ. Eph 1:1-2 (KJV)

*Paul and Timotheus, the servants of Jesus Christ, <u>to all the saints in Christ Jesus which are at Philippi</u>, with the **bishops and deacons:** Grace be unto you, and peace, from God our Father, and from the Lord Jesus Christ. Phil 1:1-2 (KJV)*
(Notice here in Philippians he says <u>bishops and deacons</u>)

Paul, an apostle of Jesus Christ by the will of God, and Timotheus our brother, <u>To the saints and faithful brethren in Christ</u> which are at Colosse: Grace be unto you, and peace, from God our Father and the Lord Jesus Christ. Col 1:1-2 (KJV)

Paul, a prisoner of Jesus Christ, and Timothy our brother, unto Philemon our dearly beloved, and fellowlabourer, And to our beloved Apphia, and Archippus our fellowsoldier, and <u>to the church in thy house:</u> Grace to you, and peace, from God our Father and the Lord Jesus Christ. Philem 1:1-3 (KJV)

James, a servant of God and of the Lord Jesus Christ, <u>to the twelve tribes</u> which are scattered abroad, greeting. James 1:1 (KJV)

Peter, an apostle of Jesus Christ, <u>to the strangers scattered</u> throughout Pontus, Galatia, Cappadocia, Asia, and Bithynia, 1 Peter 1:1 (KJV)

EK-KLĀ-SĒ'-Ä - Leadership

Jude, the servant of Jesus Christ, and brother of James, <u>to them that are sanctified by God</u> *the Father, and preserved in Jesus Christ, and called: 2 Mercy unto you, and peace, and love, be multiplied.*
Jude 1:1-2 (KJV)

If there was one man in charge of an organization it would read: *To the Bishop (or Pastor in todays church) to the church in Ephesus and the saints there greetings".* As we have pointed out previously, we are all priests unto God. That does not mean that there is no leadership but this leadership is proven mature leadership with specific qualifications.

Shepherding

There was for a brief time, a doctrine known as "shepherding" It happened in the mid 1970's and had disastrous consequences. Five leaders propagated this idea, Bob Mumford, Derek Prince, Charles Simpson, Ern Baxter and Don Bashan. Bob and Derek were early mentors for me via cassette tape. I listened to everything I could get my hands on. They saw a growing problem in the charismatic fellowships which caused them to submit themselves and their ministries to each other. They saw a need for greater accountability and deeper relationships. What started out as a good idea quickly grew into a cult like structure.

The situation was worse where there was one man in charge (the pastor). In some cases it was taken to extremes by "pastors" who felt their authority had to be obeyed by everyone under their leadership. These unruly shepherds decided that every part of a member's life had to come under their authority. This meant that the "shepherd" could tell the member to whom and when they could marry. The member could not change jobs without their blessing. In some extreme cases personal finances were taken over by these men. This has all the ear marks of a true cult. I had a small taste of that when I was moving to another city for a new job. The pastor who had accepted this belief, told me that he was not releasing me to go. After checking with my father in the faith I felt it was not rebellion to leave. That incident is mild compared to the stories I have been told by others who were under a man out of control.

Derek Prince withdrew in 1983, stating his belief that "we were guilty of the Galatian error: having begun in the Spirit, we quickly degenerated into the flesh." - from a Charisma Magazine article *Derek Prince, Charismatic Author And Bible Teacher, Dies in Jerusalem*". The January/February 1990 issue of *Ministries Today* displayed on its cover the words, "'Discipleship was wrong. I repent. I ask forgiveness.' — Bob Mumford." This disaster happened because man wanted to control the ek-klā-sē'-ä and not the Holy Spirit under the headship of Yeshua. It was a good idea gone bad by over emphasizing the authority of man. Yeshua said "But he that is greatest among you shall be your servant" Derek and Bob should not be held accountable for the extreme abuses, however others took as a license to rule over the people. Like the Holy Spirit, a good shepherd leads his sheep he does not drive them.

The Bishop (Elder, Overseer)

In Exodus 18:25, we read of Moses appointing "elders" to rule over the great congregation of Israel. The seventy ruling elders had already been chosen as the legislative body to council together with God over His Law and Commandments.

> *And Moses chose able men out of all Israel and made them heads over the people, rulers of thousands, rulers of hundreds, rulers of fifties, and rulers of tens. Exodus 18:25*

These were ranks of elders where some who were qualified were set over a thousand; while those less qualified were set over the number they could minister to. Churches today are overlooking this great ministry of the elders to the Body of Christ who are watchmen over men's souls and the spiritual life of the local churches.

Some say that the function of the "pastor" is the lead elder. I see no New Testament basis for that. The structure where you have professionally paid clergy and a single pastor who shepherds was not the norm until the 3rd or 4th century. We will discuss this in the chapter on church history. Ephesians 4:11 is the only place where the word poi-mā'n (Strong's G4166) is translated pastors, everywhere else the word is translated shepherd. Virtually, everywhere else in the New Testament it refers to Yeshua the great shepherd, except where referring to sheep herders and false shepherds. I think that we can assume that the function of a shepherd or what is called "pastor" has been greatly over emphasized! If the New Testament scripture is our guide then the churches of today do not follow a New Testament pattern for the ek-klā-sē'-ä .

Before Israel demanded a King they were ruled by Judges (one of them being Deborah a woman) These were godly men and a woman who judged righteously. I believe the elders must be able to do the same.

Basically, there are two kinds of elders. Some elders are so by example, and they have a right to counsel, while others have officially been placed in and are ruling elders or overseers of the flock as shepherds (poi-mā'n).

Elders are appointed not chosen by the congregation. It is necessary that spiritually mature individuals chose and ordain elders. These must be chosen based on prayer, the leading of the Holy Spirit and meeting the qualifications. Because a person is a leader, has a seminary degree or is popular within the fellowship does not automatically qualify them to be an elder.

> *For this cause left I thee in Crete, that thou shouldest set in order the things that are wanting, and ordain elders in every city, as I had appointed thee: Titus 1:5 (KJV)*

These elders are chosen by fasting and prayer, by the Holy Spirit and ordained by the laying on of hands:

> *Now there were in the church that was at Antioch certain prophets and teachers; as Barnabas, and Simeon that was called Niger, and Lucius of Cyrene, and Manaen, which had been brought up with Herod the tetrarch, and Saul. As they ministered to the Lord, and fasted, the Holy Ghost said, Separate me Barnabas and Saul for the work whereunto I have called them. And when they had fasted and prayed, and laid their hands on them, they sent them away. Acts 13:1-3 (KJV)*

I have seen many people "ordained" by organizations simply because they completed a course of study or for other reasons of their own. That is appropriate if the intent is being able to conduct marriage ceremonies but it does not guarantee that they have been selected by the Holy Spirit to shepherd the ek-klā-sē'-ä . This is a dangerous practice. Anyone can get ordination papers but only a few are selected by the Holy Spirit to shepherd the flock. It is very similar to what I experienced in the business world. I found that sometimes those with the degree were less productive than those with no degree. Because it is not the paper certificate that makes one productive it is the quality of the person. Please do not think I am saying that education is useless, far from it, I regularly check what I believe with those who have a formal education. But having a paper that says you are qualified does not make you so.

I think of the Azusa Street revival and the ensuing Pentecostal movement. The traditional church ridiculed them for being poor and uneducated. And yet, the word tells us that the Lord chooses what the world calls foolish to confound the wise. Why? So that no flesh should glory in itself. It does not say that He chooses no mighty only that he chose few.

> *For ye see your calling, brethren, how that not many wise men after the flesh, not many mighty, not many noble, are called: But God hath chosen the foolish things of the world to confound the wise; and God hath chosen the weak things of the world to confound the things which are mighty; And base things of the world, and things which are despised, hath God chosen, yea, and things which are not, to bring to nought things that are: That no flesh should glory in his presence. But of him are ye in Christ Jesus, who of God is made unto us wisdom, and righteousness, and sanctification, and redemption: That, according as it is written, He that glorieth, let him glory in the Lord. 1 Corinthians 1:26-31 (KJV)*

I started on a quest to obtain a PhD in theology thinking this would give me credibility since I was writing a book typically written by those with the advanced degrees. I started the program. One day while driving and seeking the Lord, the Holy Spirit asked me why I was pursuing this degree. As I thought about the degree, it occurred to me, getting the title would grant credibility by the world's standard but would that bring glory to the Lord? **Please** do not think I am saying that pursuing a degree of any type is ungodly, it is not. For me being called Doctor or having PhD after my name would be a matter of pride. I quit pursuing the degree. I found that everything I would learn in a formal setting was available in self study. The Internet and electronic media has opened a whole world that was not available years ago. I have found complete university courses on-line, and many resources that would have been too costly not long ago. It was up to me to dig for the truth, to learn everything I could by the leading of the and by Holy Spirit, checking and cross checking what was being taught.

> *Then he answered and spake unto me, saying, This is the word of the Lord unto Zerubbabel, saying, Not by might, nor by power, but by my spirit, saith the Lord of hosts. Zechariah 4:6 (KJV)*

The Lord does not want us to rely on our own wisdom and craftiness but upon Him and the leading of the Holy Spirit. We read over and over again where complete dependence on the Lord leads to victory but dependence on ourselves or others ends in defeat.

When I was twenty, I spent hours studying the word and seeking the Lord. One day I heard the Holy Spirit speak to me: "I want you to teach but I do not want you to go to seminary to become a teacher". My assumption was that he wanted to teach me. That did not mean that I was not to be mentored by great leaders. I spent my early years voraciously devouring the Word and listening to the teaching of Bob Mumford, Derek Prince and other great leaders of the day. I still listen to great teachers today. I don't always agree with everything that is said but I check it out for myself to confirm or deny what is being taught, I recommend you do the same.

> *But the anointing which ye have received of him abideth in you, and ye need not that any man teach you: but as the same anointing teacheth you of all things, and is truth, and is no lie, and even as it hath taught you, ye shall abide in him. 1 John 2:27 (KJV)*

Qualifications of an Elder/Bishop:

There are three words for this office, Bishop, Overseer and Elder.
1 Timothy 3:1-7 (KJV)
This is a true saying, If a man desire the office of a bishop, he desireth a good work. It is important here that the person wants the responsibility and is not coerced in to the position.

A bishop then must be:

1. blameless, - Expositors[4] says: "It is not enough for him to be not criminal; he must be one against whom it is impossible to bring any charge of wrong doing such as could stand impartial examination. He must be without reproach.

2. the husband of one wife, - Wuest word studies[5] explains it this way: Now, to consider the meaning of the words, "the husband of one wife." The Greek is mias (one) gunaikos (woman) andra (man). The word "man" is not anthrōpos, the generic term for man, but anēr, the term used of a male individual of the human race. The other two words are in the genitive case, while anēr is in the accusative. The literal translation is, "a man of one woman." The words, when used of the marriage relation come to mean, "a husband of one wife." The two nouns are without the definite article, which construction emphasizes character or nature. The entire context is one in which the character of the bishop is being discussed. Thus, one can translate, "a one-wife sort of a husband," or "a one-woman sort of a man." We speak of the Airedale as a one-man dog. We mean by that, that it is his nature to become attached to only one man, his master. Since character is emphasized by the Greek construction, the bishop should be a man who loves only one woman as his wife.

The following definitions are from Thayers Greek Testament[6]

3. vigilant, νηφάλιος nay-fal'-eh-os sober, temperate

4. sober, σώφρων sōphrōn of a sound mind, sane, in one's senses

5. of good behaviour, κόσμιος kosmios - well arranged, seemly, modest

6. given to hospitality, φιλόξενος philoxenos hospitable, generous to guests

7. apt to teach; διδακτικός didaktikos apt and skillful in teaching

8. Not given to wine, πάροινος paroinos given to wine, drunken

9. no striker, πλήκτης plēktēs contentious, quarrelsome person

10. not greedy of filthy lucre; but patient, αἰσχροκερδής aischrokerdēs - greedy for money

11. not a brawler, ἄμαχος amachos abstaining from fighting

12. *not covetous;* ἀφιλάργυρος aphilarguros not loving money,

13. *One that ruleth well his own house,* *having his children in subjection with all gravity; (For if a man know not how to rule his own house, how shall he take care of the church of God?)*

14. *Not a novice,* νεόφυτος neophutos a new convert, neophyte (one who has recently become a Christian)
lest being lifted up with pride he fall into the condemnation of the devil.

15. *Moreover he* must have a good report *of them which are without; lest he fall into reproach and the snare of the devil.*
"In the passage before us, indeed, St. Paul may be understood to imply that the opinion of 'those without' might usefully balance or correct that of the Church. There is something blameworthy in a man's character if the consensus of outside opinion be unfavorable to him; no matter how much he may be admired and respected by his own party. Expositors[4]

Overseer

The verbal form is episkopeō, "to look over, to oversee, to superintend, to exercise oversight or care over." The word came originally from secular life, referring to the foreman of a construction gang, or the supervisor of building construction, for instance. Thayer defines the word; "an overseer, a man charged with the duty of seeing that things to be done by others are done rightly, any curator, guardian, or superintendent." The word was taken up by the Church, and designated an overseer of any Christian church. The responsibilities of this office have to do with the oversight and direction of the spiritual life of the local church. Wuest Word Studies[5]

The word overseer is G1984. ἐπισκοπή episkopē; g, to look after. Visitation, or the public office of an overseer (epískopos [G1985]). The act of visiting or being visited, inspected. Zodhiates[7]

Elder

Presbuteros, "an elder," is another term for the same person as bishop or overseer. See Act 20:17 with verse Act 20:28. The term "elder" indicates the mature spiritual experience and understanding of those so described; the term "bishop," or "overseer," indicates the character of the work undertaken. According to the Divine will and appointment, as in the NT, there were to be "bishops" in every local church, Act 14:23; Act 20:17; Phi 1:1; Tit 1:5; Jam 5:14. Where the singular is used, the passage is describing what a "bishop" should be, 1Ti 3:2; Tit 1:7. Christ Himself is spoken of as "the ... Bishop of our souls," 1Pe 2:25. - Mounce[8]

Elders are a part of a local fellowship. The function of an apostle on the other hand is not, they are sent out. It is the responsibility of the Elders to shepherd the local flock. In many cases ,we learn that Paul planted a local fellowship and then may stay with them for some time to ground and establish them. But then, always turned the oversight of the group to the Elders. Since "apostle" is a function and not a title, Peter would be an apostle when he was sent out and an elder when he was at home.

> *The elders which are among you I exhort, who am also an elder, and a witness of the sufferings of Christ, and also a partaker of the glory that shall be revealed: Feed the flock of God which is among you, taking the oversight thereof, not by constraint, but willingly; not for filthy lucre, but of a ready mind; Neither as being lords over God's heritage, but being ensamples to the flock. And when the chief Shepherd shall appear, ye shall receive a crown of glory that fadeth not away. 1 Peter 5:1-4 (KJV)*

Post-apostolic bishops of importance include Polycarp of Smyrna, Ignatius of Antioch and Clement of Rome . These men reportedly knew and studied under the apostles personally and are therefore called Apostolic Fathers. Their writings would not be considered scripture but we can gain some insight by reading what they taught as well as understanding the error taught by the Gnostics, whom they exposed.

> **Chapter VI.—The duties of presbyters and others.**
> And let the presbyters be compassionate and merciful to all, bringing back those that wander, visiting all the sick, and not neglecting the widow, the orphan, or the poor, but always

"providing for that which is becoming in the sight of God and man;" abstaining from all wrath, respect of persons, and unjust judgment; keeping far off from all covetousness, not quickly crediting [an evil report] against any one, not severe in judgment, as knowing that we are all under a debt of sin.
Polycarp (a disciple of John)- *Epistle to the Philippians*

There is a man who I believe exemplified all the qualifications of an elder: William Gay. He did not need to be given the title because he was an elder in every respect. If the church where he was initially an elder would have truly structured its fellowship after the New Testament pattern of co-leadership, a lot of problems would have been avoided. He was wise, he had a genuine love for the people. Even though he had a full time job, he never turned anyone away day or night who needed counseling or help. I believe that more people came to Bill and his wife Shirley than to the so called pastor of that fellowship. Young people, myself included would find ourselves drawn to meet at his house. Shirley was equally qualified and gave of herself way beyond the call of duty and still does to this day. In fact there is no one else I know who exemplified the purest example of service to others in this world. She would be someone who we should all follow as an example of what it means to be a true Christian, a servant and a leader.

In Acts we hear that "they had all things in common" this was true of Bill and Shirley. They shared whatever they had with anyone who had a need, regardless of whether they got any thanks in return. I can tell you first hand that this life was genuine because I lived with them for several years. I left home when I was 15 and met Bill and Shirley when I was 20. I would not be here today if I had not been discipled by them. This is what the ek-klā-sē'-ä should be about today.

Please be careful about having all things in common, giving when it is "coerced" is a red flag that should warn of something not right. Evil shepherds are those which lead people into error by control. One technique used by our enemy is to mix truth with error. Be sure that you know what an organization truly believes before you get involved. You would agree with a lot of what the Jehovah Witnesses say, and also what other cults believe. That is the hook of those who are heretics and cults, quote enough truth to get someone to agree and then subtly interject bits of heresy. If

EK-KLĀ-SĒ'-Ä - Leadership

you are not equipped by your fellowship to recognize these groups or to know the Word yourself, then leave, and go somewhere where you will be equipped, this equipping is one purpose of the ek-klā-sē'-ä . We are living in the age of apostasy. There will be a falling away do not be one of those who falls away. Be prepared for what is coming. Yeshua talks about not being deceived three times in 9 verses in Matthew 24:4-13

> *And Jesus answered and said unto them, Take heed that no man* **deceive you***. For many shall come in my name, saying, I am Christ; and shall* **deceive many***. And ye shall hear of wars and rumours of wars: see that ye be not troubled: for all these things must come to pass, but the end is not yet. For nation shall rise against nation, and kingdom against kingdom: and there shall be famines, and pestilences, and earthquakes, in divers places. All these are the beginning of sorrows. Then shall they deliver you up to be afflicted, and shall kill you: and ye shall be hated of all nations for my name's sake. And then shall many be offended, and shall betray one another, and shall hate one another. And many false prophets shall rise,* **and shall deceive many***. And because iniquity shall abound, the love of many shall wax cold. But he that shall endure unto the end, the same shall be saved. Matt 24:4-13*

It is the duty of the Elders (Overseers, Bishops) to shepherd the flock, to watch over them, and protect them from false teachers, prophets and the wolves that come into the flock to destroy it. This usually happens when there is gossip, false witnesses, and slight error in prophecy and teaching. The Elders and the servants of the people, are there to serve, NOT to be served.

After having completed this book, I came across an excellent book which explores the role of the elder in great detail: *Biblical Eldership and Urgent Call To Restore Biblical Church Leadership* by Alexander Strauch. He confirmed what I believe about leadership in the church. I am including a brief quote from his book in this second edition.

Speaking about the current church-board style of leadership Strauch says:

> One does not need to read Greek or be professionally trained in theology to understand that the contemporary, church-

board concept of eldership is irreconcilably at odds with the New Testament definition of eldership. According to the New Testament concept of eldership, elders lead the church, teach and preach the Word, protect the church from false teachers, exhort and admonish the saints in sound doctrine, visit the sick and pray, and judge doctrinal issues.

To be an elder requires that you be more than a casual member who attends board meetings. Each elder should be the equivalent of what we recognize as a pastor role today. To effectively lead, the biblical elder is committing himself to the flock. This is not a part-time commitment, it means taking on responsibility for the care and feeding of those they shepherd. Shepherd is a good word for what the elder does for the flock. That is not to say that the elder has to be a full-time paid position. It does mean that they are on call 24/7, not unlike doctors were when they used to make house calls. To be a New Testament elder requires a huge commitment and should not be entered into haphazardly. The days of one man completely in charge need to come to an end, if we are to truly follow the teaching of the New Testament.

Deacons

And in these days when the number of the disciples was multiplying, there arose a low, undertone murmuring of the Hellenists who were conferring together, secretly complaining against the Hebrews, the complaint being that their widows were being neglected in the daily provision of food. Then the Twelve, having called to themselves the entire number of the disciples, said, It is not fitting that we should neglect the word of God, to be occupied with the distribution of food. Now, look, brethren, for men from among yourselves who are accredited, seven of them, controlled by the Spirit and filled with broad and full intelligence whom we shall appoint over this business. But as for us, to prayer and the ministry of the Word we shall give constant attention. Acts 6:1-4 (Wuest)

Likewise the deacons must be
      1. *grave,*
      2. *not double tongued,*
      3. *not given to much wine,*
      4. *not greedy of filthy lucre;*
      5. *Holding the mystery of the faith in a pure conscience.*

EK-KLĀ-SĒ'-Ä - Leadership

And **let these also first be proved**; *then let them use the office of a deacon, being found blameless. Even so must their wives be grave, not slanderers, sober, faithful in all things. Let the deacons be the husbands of one wife, ruling their children and their own houses well. For they that have used the office of a deacon well purchase to themselves a good degree, and great boldness in the faith which is in Christ Jesus.*

The absence of the article before "deacons" shows that these church officers, charged with the temporal welfare of the local church as the bishops were with its spiritual welfare, are treated as a class. The Greek word is used generally of a servant as seen from the standpoint of his activity in service. Wuest Word Studies[5]

> G1249. διάκονος diákonos; gen. diakónou, masc., fem. noun. A minister, servant, deacon. The derivation is uncertain. According to some it comes from diakónis, in the dust laboring, or running through dust. Others derive it from diákō, the same as diēkō, to hasten, related to diōkō, to pursue. Also used in the NT as a technical term side by side with epískopos (G1985), bishop or overseer (1 Tim. 3:8, 12; Phil. 1:1). The deacons in this sense were helping or serving the bishops or elders, and this is why they were probably called deacons. They did not, though, possess any ruling authority as did the elders. Tychicus was called a deacon in his relation to Paul (Eph. 6:21; Col. 4:7 [cf. Acts 19:22]). The origin of this relationship is likely found in Acts 6:1- 4. Stephen and Philip were deacons and were first chosen as distributors of alms and other forms of aid, but soon appeared alongside the Apostles and as their helpers and as evangelists (Acts 6:8- 10; 8:5- 8). The care of the churches fell upon the deacons as the helpers of the elders who held distinct offices. – Zodhiates[7]

> one who renders service to another; a deacon or deaconess, whose official duty was to superintend the alms of the Church, with other kindred services, Rom. 16:1; Phil. 1:1; 1 Tim. 3:8, 12 - Mounce[8]

Polycarp gives us some insight into what was expected of a deacon in his letter to the Phillipians:

> *Chapter V.—The duties of deacons, youths, and virgins.*
> Knowing, then, that "God is not mocked," we ought to walk worthy of His commandment and glory. In like manner should the deacons be blameless before the face of His righteousness, as being the servants of God and Christ, and not of men. They must not be slanderers, double-tongued, or lovers of money, but temperate in all things, compassionate, industrious, walking according to the truth of the Lord, who was the servant of all. If we please Him in this present world, we shall receive also the future world, according as He has promised to us that He will raise us again from the dead, and that if we live worthily of Him, "we shall also reign together with Him," provided only we believe. In like manner, let the young men also be blameless in all things, being especially careful to preserve purity, and keeping themselves in, as with a bridle, from every kind of evil. For it is well that they should be cut off from the lusts that are in the world, since "every lust warreth against the spirit;" and "neither fornicators, nor effeminate, nor abusers of themselves with mankind, shall inherit the kingdom of God," nor those who do things inconsistent and unbecoming. **_Wherefore, it is needful to abstain from all these things, being subject to the presbyters and deacons, as unto God and Christ_**. The virgins also must walk in a blameless and pure conscience.

There are many things we could discuss from this text but I would like to point out that he says **"being subject to the presbyters and deacons, as unto God and Christ"** He did not say be subject to the pastor and the elders. Again we have evidence from the early church that the leadership structure was not like it is today.

Other functions in a New Testament ek-klā-sē'-ä

> *Now ye are the body of Christ, and members in particular. And God hath set some in the church, first apostles, secondarily prophets, thirdly teachers, after that miracles, then gifts of healings, helps, governments, diversities of tongues. 1 Corinthians 12:27-28*

We are all members of one body. Each one has a role and a purpose. Remember what Paul said in 1 Corinthians just prior to the above verse that each member of the body is necessary. The members who have a more obvious position should not get more honor than those with less. All parts are necessary for the operation of the body.

> *For as the body is one, and hath many members, and all the members of that one body, being many, are one body: so also is Christ. For by one Spirit are we all baptized into one body, whether we be Jews or Gentiles, whether we be bond or free; and have been all made to drink into one Spirit. For the body is not one member, but many. If the foot shall say, Because I am not the hand, I am not of the body; is it therefore not of the body? And if the ear shall say, Because I am not the eye, I am not of the body; is it therefore not of the body? If the whole body were an eye, where were the hearing? If the whole were hearing, where were the smelling? But now hath God set the members every one of them in the body, as it hath pleased him. And if they were all one member, where were the body? But now are they many members, yet but one body. And the eye cannot say unto the hand, I have no need of thee: nor again the head to the feet, I have no need of you. Nay, much more those members of the body, which seem to be more feeble, are necessary: And those members of the body, which we think to be less honourable, upon these we bestow more abundant honour; and our uncomely parts have more abundant comeliness. For our comely parts have no need: but God hath tempered the body together, having given more abundant honour to that part which lacked: That there should be no schism in the body; but that the members should have the same care one for another. And whether one member suffer, all the members suffer with it; or one member be honoured, all the members rejoice with it.*
> 1 Corinthians 12:12-26 (KJV)

We must realize that there are many parts to the body some are more visible than others but each one is essential! Please remember that just because a ministry is more visible to us does not mean that it is more important or more critical. We look at the outside, but the Lord looks at the inside, remember the widow and her mite, she gave more than the self-righteous. Don't ever think that because the teacher, apostle or prophet are very visible functions that they are storing up more treasures in heaven. The Lord's judgment is nothing like ours. My conjecture is that some of these visible ministries may have their reward already. Never assume that your part in the body is not as valuable as any other part. If we look at the body from a physical sense what do we discover.

Eyes - How would we recognize a need if we could not see?
Ears - How could we get revelation from the Holy Spirit if we could not hear?
Nose - How could we smell trouble when it is coming?
Mouth - How could we tell others about the good news?
Limbs - How could we walk, work or serve?

But now hath God set the members every one of them in the body, **as it hath pleased him**. *And if they were all one member, where were the body?*

The analogy of the Ek-klā-sē'-ä being a body is a good one. There are critical parts of the body that are not so obvious. No one can see your liver, but it is critical to life because it cleanses the harmful tocsins out of your system. You can not see the lungs, but it brings life giving oxygen to your cells. If we were to analyze it carefully, we may find that any healthy fellowship has all of its parts operating. When the body breaks down the immune system kick in and does its job. If you get a cold or the flu your entire body suffers, it is the same in the Ek-klā-sē'-ä.

Paul does not give us a lot detail about the less visible ministries so I will speculate.

Intercessors - I believe because of the persistent intercession of my grandmother, that I was given many opportunities to know the Lord. This is a function that is desperately needed in the Ek-klā-sē'-ä today. There are some groups which meet every week to do just that. I am sure they can tell you how many times their intercession was successful. I am aware of one dramatic story of a man called Earthquake Kelly. (I recommend his book *Bound to Lose Destined to Win*) Read of his near-death experiences, after dying of a drug overdose at age fifteen he was being pulled into hell, but because his mother was interceding at the time he was spared.

Do not underestimate the power of intercession. Although very likely overlooked and misunderstood this ministry is vital for a healthy body. If you are called to this ministry, please do not neglect it, the rest of the body depends on it.

> The second truth which I have sought to enforce is that we have far too little conception of the place that intercession, as distinguished from prayer for ourselves, ought to have in the Church and the Christian life. In intercession our King upon the throne finds His highest glory; in it we shall find our highest glory too. Through it He continues His saving work, and can do nothing without it; through it alone we can do our work, and nothing avails without it. In it He ever receives from the Father the Holy Spirit and all spiritual blessings to impart; in it we too are called to receive in ourselves the fullness of God's Spirit, with the power to impart spiritual blessing to others. The power of the Church truly to bless rests on intercession—asking and receiving heavenly gifts to carry to men. Because this is so, it is no wonder that where, owing to lack of teaching or spiritual insight, we [p6] trust in our own diligence and effort, to the influence of the world and the flesh, and work more than we pray, the presence and power of God are not seen in our work as we would wish.
>
> Andrew Murray.
> *The Ministry of Intercession / A Plea for More Prayer*

Everyone should be engaged in some way. **Christianity is not a spectator sport.** We are all required to know the Word and the Lord on our own not vicariously through another.

Women in the Ek-klā-sē'-ä

This is a subject of much controversy. I do not claim to have the answer here, we can only go by what the word says. Do we fully understand all the ramifications of what Paul is saying? I am not sure, you must come to your own conclusion.

We do know that the gnostics allowed women to hold the highest offices mainly based on their belief that the Holy Spirit was female.

In today's modern church women are taking roles of authority as Bishops and Teachers. I do not see anywhere in the New Testament where women are given places of authority over men. That does not mean they are any less than their male counterpart. There are many things that women can do in the New Testament ek-klā-sē'-ä : they can be deacons, pray, prophecy, teach younger women, ... just not have governmental authority over men.

> *And the Lord God said, It is not good that the man should be alone; I will make him an help meet for him. Genesis 2:18 (KJV)*

> *"A bishop then must be blameless, the **husband** of one wife, vigilant, sober, of good behaviour, given to hospitality, apt to teach... One that **ruleth well his own house**, having his children in subjection with all gravity; (For if a man know not how to rule his own house, how shall he take care of the church of God?) 1 Timothy 3: 2,4-5*

> *"Let the woman learn in silence with all subjection. But I suffer not a woman **to teach**, nor to **usurp authority over the man**, but to be in silence." 1 Timothy 2: 11-12*

usurp authority: Strongs's G831. αὐθεντέω authenteō; to use or exercise authority or power over as an autocrat, to domineer. - Zodhiathies[7]

In the earlier usage of the word it signified one who with his own hand killed either others or himself. Later it came to denote one who acts on his own "authority;" hence, "to exercise authority, dominion." - Vines[9]

> *Wives, submit yourselves unto your own husbands, as unto the Lord. For the husband is the head of the wife, even as Christ is the head of the church: and he is the saviour of the body. 2Therefore as the church is subject unto Christ, so let the wives be to their own husbands in every thing. Husbands, love your wives, even as Christ*

also loved the church, and gave himself for it; Ephesians 5:22-25

Likewise, ye wives, be in subjection to your own husbands; that, if any obey not the word, they also may without the word be won by the conversation of the wives; While they behold your chaste conversation coupled with fear. Whose adorning let it not be that outward adorning of plaiting the hair, and of wearing of gold, or of putting on of apparel; But let it be the hidden man of the heart, in that which is not corruptible, even the ornament of a meek and quiet spirit, which is in the sight of God of great price. For after this manner in the old time the holy women also, who trusted in God, adorned themselves, being in subjection unto their own husbands: Even as Sara obeyed Abraham, calling him lord: whose daughters ye are, as long as ye do well, and are not afraid with any amazement. Likewise, ye husbands, dwell with them according to knowledge, giving honour unto the wife, as unto the weaker vessel, and as being heirs together of the grace of life; that your prayers be not hindered. 1 Peter 3:1-7 (KJV)

Let your women keep silence in the churches: for it is not permitted unto them to <u>speak</u>; but they are commanded to be under obedience, as also saith the law. And if they will learn any thing, let them ask their husbands at home: for it is a shame for women to speak in the church. 1 Cor 14:34-35 (KJV)

<u>Speak:</u> Strong's G2980. λαλέω laléō; To talk at random, as contrasted with légō (G3004) which involves the intellectual part of man, his reason. It is used especially of children with the meaning of to talk much. Zodhaites[7]

I will state a generalization, it is true that some women do have a tendency to talk at random about many things and can go on for sometime. Many times I have said to my wife "get to the point" because in some there is a tendency to ramble. Is this what Paul is referring to? We don't have enough information here to make a solid case. Based on the context, I believe Paul is saying that women should not ramble or talk too much as to take over a meeting. There is something that we are not told in this verse, it is assumed that we know the culture of time and what the real problem was in this situation. I do not believe that women were never to say anything. We may never know what the issue was Paul was correcting.

When the older women teach the younger ones it is based on experience that has been gained over time. Most of what a young woman may face has most likely been faced by the aged women. They have a better understanding than any man would. Young girls today are ill-equipped to face married life and it is possible that this is why we have so many divorces in the church. Is it because young women are not equipped to face the ups and downs of a marriage?

> *The **aged women** likewise, that they be in behaviour as becometh holiness, not false accusers, not given to much wine, teachers of good things; That **they may teach the young women** to be sober, to love their husbands, to love their children, To be discreet, chaste, keepers at home, good, obedient to their own husbands, that the word of God be not blasphemed.*
> *Titus 2:3-5 (KJV)*

> *But I would have you know, that the head of every man is Christ; and the head of the woman is the man; and the head of Christ is God. Every man praying or prophesying, having his head covered, dishonoureth his head. But every woman that prayeth or prophesieth with her head uncovered dishonoureth her head: for that is even all one as if she were shaven. For if the woman be not covered, let her also be shorn: but if it be a shame for a woman to be shorn or shaven, let her be covered. For a man indeed ought not to cover his head, forasmuch as he is the image and glory of God: but the woman is the glory of the man. For the man is not of the woman; but the woman of the man. Neither was the man created for the woman; but the woman for the man. For this cause ought the woman to have power on her head because of the angels. Nevertheless neither is the man without the woman, neither the woman without the man, in the Lord. For as the woman is of the man, even so is the man also by the woman; but all things of God. Judge in yourselves: is it comely that a woman pray unto God uncovered? Doth not even nature itself teach you, that, if a man have long hair, it is a shame unto him? But if a woman have long hair, it is a glory to her: for her hair is given her for a covering. But if any man seem to be contentious, we have no such custom, neither the churches of God. 1 Corinthians 11:3-16 (KJV)*

EK-KLĀ-SĒ'-Ä - Leadership

Women are not to teach or baptize.

> But if the writings which wrongly go under Paul's name, claim Thecla's example as a licence for women's teaching and baptizing, let them know that, in Asia, the presbyter who composed that writing, (The allusion is to a spurious work entitled *Acta Pauli et Theclæ*) as if he were augmenting Paul's fame from his own store, after being convicted, and confessing that he had done it from love of Paul, was removed from his office. For how credible would it seem, that he who has not permitted a woman even to learn with over-boldness, should give a female the power of teaching and of baptizing! "Let them be silent," he says, "and at home consult their own husbands."
> Tertullian. *Chapter XVII.—Of the Power of Conferring Baptism*

There are many women of old who were held in high esteem.

> Many women also, being strengthened by the grace of God, have performed numerous manly exploits. The blessed Judith, when her city was besieged, asked of the elders permission to go forth into the camp of the strangers; and, exposing herself to danger, she went out for the love which she bare to her country and people then besieged; and the Lord delivered *Holofernes into the hands of a woman. Clement of Rome - *The First Epistle to the Cornthians Chapter 55 - Examples of such Love*
>
> * "Approaching to his bed, she took hold of the hair of his head, and said, Strengthen me, O Lord God of Israel, this day! And she smote twice upon his neck with all her might, and she took away his head from him." (Judith, 13:7-8 included in the Septuagint but not in the Christian Bible).

If you are observant you will see that women in general are more sensitive than men to things spiritual. This is the good and bad news. They accept Yeshua more readily than men and in the case of my wife she can hear the Lord speak clearer and quicker than I do. When she hears a word from the Lord she is always right, so I rely on her. That is the good side of the of the issue. The bad side is that since they are more spiritually in tune they can be lead astray by feelings and emotions. There is a reason that women should have a covering. Paul says that the head of man is Yeshua and the head of a woman is the man.

> *But I would have you know, that the head of every man is Christ; and the head of the woman is the man; and the head of Christ is God.* 1 Corinthians 11:3 (KJV)

It is not just a matter of wives submitting to their husbands but it is the duty of the husband to love the wife as Christ loved the church.

> *Submitting yourselves one to another in the fear of God. Wives, submit yourselves unto your own husbands, as unto the Lord. For the husband is the head of the wife, even as Christ is the head of the church: and he is the saviour of the body. Therefore as the church is subject unto Christ, so let the wives be to their own husbands in every thing. Husbands, love your wives, even as Christ also loved the church, and gave himself for it;* Ephesians 5:21-25 (KJV)

There is something that happened in the garden that is not clear but Paul makes reference to the fact that it was the woman that was deceived and not Adam. It is this reason that women are not to rule over men in a governmental position. Please remember that women do have many ministries and are quite effective more so than men in some cases. But being an Overseer is not one of them.

> *Let the woman learn in silence with all subjection. But I suffer not a woman to teach, nor to usurp authority over the man, but to be in silence. For Adam was first formed, then Eve. And Adam was not deceived, but the woman being deceived was in the transgression* 1 Timothy 2:11-14 (KJV)

The 4 fold Ministry

We won't split hairs here call it 5 if you like but strictly speaking as we have already discussed there are only four functions. The Greek grammar would tell you there are only four because Paul says *some, apostles; and some, prophets; and some, evangelists; and some, pastors and teachers;* Notice that the pastor is linked with teacher. This would make perfect sense because the elders are the pastors, the shepherds who watch over the flock. One of the qualifications of an elder is "apt to teach" **didaktikos** apt and skillful in teaching. Nowhere in God's Word do we find anyone referred to as a shepherd (pastor). This confirms the fact that shepherds and teachers are one class of men. It also makes the case that there is not a pastor (singular) but Pastors / Teachers, Shepherds, Overseers. In the modern church we find almost universally a single man named Pastor. How far we have come from the early New Testament pattern for church government.

> *There is one body, and one Spirit, even as ye are called in one hope of your calling; One Lord, one faith, one baptism, One God and Father of all, who is above all, and through all, and in you all. But unto every one of us is given grace according to the measure of the gift of Christ. Wherefore he saith, When he ascended up on high, he led captivity captive, and gave gifts unto men. (Now that he ascended, what is it but that he also descended first into the lower parts of the earth? He that descended is the same also that ascended up far above all heavens, that he might fill all things.) And he gave some, apostles; and some, prophets; and some, evangelists; and some, pastors and teachers; For the perfecting of the saints, for the work of the ministry, for the edifying of the body of Christ: Till we all come in the unity of the faith, and of the knowledge of the Son of God, unto a perfect man, unto the measure of the stature of the fulness of Christ: That we henceforth be no more children, tossed to and fro, and carried about with every wind of doctrine, by the sleight of men, and cunning craftiness, whereby they lie in wait to deceive; But speaking the truth in love, may grow up into him in all things, which is the head, even Christ: From whom the whole body fitly joined together and compacted by that which every joint supplieth, according to the effectual working in the measure of every part, maketh increase of the body unto the edifying of itself in love. Ephesians 4:4-16 (KJV)*

Now ye are the body of Christ, and members in particular. And God hath set some in the church, first apostles, secondarily prophets, thirdly teachers, after that miracles, then gifts of healings, helps, governments, diversities of tongues. 1 Corinthians 12:27-28 (KJV)

These are functions **NOT** titles, by making these definitions titles, we subject the wearer with an unfair burden to perfectly perform according to preconceived ideas based on traditions of men. Rather if it is seen as functions that are carried out by the one operating in that function at the time there would be less confusion. In my mind the old saying makes sense. "If it looks like a duck, sounds like a duck and acts like a duck it is most likely a duck". Putting a sign around the neck of a chicken that reads: "I am a Duck" does not make it so...

Getting certification, ordination or a university degree does not qualify someone to do the work for which they have been certified. It has been my experience that "titles" have little or nothing to do with the quality of the person wearing the "badge" or title. We have professionals who are called "pastors" simply because they have finished a course of study at a seminary or have be "ordained" by some organization. They have knowledge but knowledge is a dangerous thing, they have the papers but without practical experience and daily walking with the Lord who saved them. They may have potential but their potential will not be instantly realized upon ordination or graduation.

In one case a "pastor" came out of seminar and immediately took over a church. This man had no practical experience and had not held a job where he had to provide for a family. Because of that he had no understanding or empathy for those who did and would make impractical demands on their time. It is my belief that if a fellowship is small, less than 150 people or so, there should not be any full-time paid leadership and there should always be more than one person capable of leading and teaching. Before putting someone in a Leadership position they must always be tested and then only by the confirmation by the Holy Spirit with fasting and prayer.

I am not saying that all of these recently ordained are disqualified, only that the "sheepskin", certificate does not qualify a person to fully function in one of these titles. We only have to look at the denominational churches today to see the effect of those who are not ordained by the Lord to see the destructive force of that kind of ordination. Many today deny the authority of the Word and some deny The Messiah.

I hear people say "he is an Apostle" giving the person a title of apostle when in fact that title may have been granted by men. In some churches I see badges announcing that the person wearing the display is an apostle or a prophet. If you have to wear a badge to announce the fact that you are a "whatever" you most likely are not. There are people who may at one time or another function as an Apostle and at other times function as a shepherd or a teacher. To me the only thing we should wear is a life that tells others we are a bond slave of Christ. People should recognize the function not the person. If someone calls themselves a prophet and does not accurately bring forth truth then I believe we can ignore the title. The early apostolic fathers would call anyone who did not accurately prophesy 100% of the time a false prophet.

We have people in the Pulpit (with certifications and ordination) today who deny Christ.

> *But there were false prophets also among the people, even as there shall be false teachers among you, who privily shall bring in damnable heresies, even denying the Lord that bought them, and bring upon themselves swift destruction. 2 Peter 2:1 (KJV)*

Not Who but What

These titles describe a function. People can move from one to another as the need arises. Just like the gifts of the Spirit. The Holy Spirit gives them as He wills... When will these functions cease? When we all come in the unity of the faith.

> *But unto every one of us is given grace according to the measure of the gift of Christ. Wherefore he saith, When he ascended up on high, he led captivity captive, and gave gifts unto men. (Now that he ascended, what is it but that he also descended first into the lower parts of the earth? He that descended is the same also that ascended up far above all heavens, that he might fill all things.) And he gave some, apostles; and some, prophets; and some,*

evangelists; and some, pastors and teachers; For the perfecting of the saints, for the work of the ministry, for the edifying of the body of Christ: **<u>Till we all come in the unity of the faith, and of the knowledge of the Son of God, unto a perfect man, unto the measure of the stature of the fullness of Christ:</u>** *That we henceforth be no more children, tossed to and fro, and carried about with every wind of doctrine, by the sleight of men, and cunning craftiness, whereby they lie in wait to deceive; But speaking the truth in love, may grow up into him in all things, which is the head, even Christ: From whom the whole body fitly joined together and compacted by that which every joint supplieth, according to the effectual working in the measure of every part, maketh increase of the body unto the edifying of itself in love. Ephesians 4:7-16 (KJV)*

I do not think we have reached that point yet, do you?

Apostles

Apostles is, literally., "one sent forth" (apo, "from," stello, "to send") – Vines Expository Dictionary[9]. The Apostle then is generally not one confined to a local assembly. They are sent out to other groups for various reasons.

Apostle Broadly refers to a "messenger, delegate," or "sent one." In classical Greek, apostolos referred to a person of merit sent as an envoy or on behalf of a master in an administrative role. John uses the term in a similar way, applying it to any messenger without the specific idea of an office with special status (Jn. 13:16). The call to apostleship is not initiated by the human agent but by God in Jesus Christ alone (Gal. 1:1) and comes about through meeting the risen Lord (1 Cor. 9:1; 15,7; Gal. 1:16). (b) Suffering is a mark of apostleship (1 Cor. 4:9- 13; 2 Cor. 4:7- 12; 11,23- 29). (c) Like the OT prophets, apostles have special insight into the mysteries of God (1 Cor. 4:1). (d) Apostolic authority is not the result of inherent quality in the office holder but is a function of the gospel's own power to convict and communicate truth (Rom. 15:18; 2 Cor. 4:2). - Mounce Complete Expository Dictionary Of New Testament Words[8]

EK-KLĀ-SĒ'-Ä - Leadership

In a strict sense there were only 12 original apostles. One, Judas was replaced. Some say that after the first century there were no longer any apostles. But as "one sent forth" the function of an apostle could continue throughout time.

Since we are far removed from the original 12 and the apostle Paul it is difficult to say what an apostle would be today in a New Testament fellowship. Are there apostles today? I would say yes in the sense that there are those who are sent out and travel from place to place setting up churches and teaching sound doctrine. If a fellowship is established they would come under the authority of the local leadership and teach and inspire the local body of believers. If these apostles were to follow example of Paul they would; lay foundational truths, after prayer and fasting appoint deacons and elders, be available to the fellowship as a resource and correct any error in thinking or practice.

Paul and Barnabas

> *Which when the apostles, Barnabas and Paul, heard of, they rent their clothes, and ran in among the people, crying out Acts 14:14*

> *Paul, a servant of Jesus Christ, called to be an apostle, separated unto the gospel of God, Romans 1:1*

> *As they ministered to the Lord, and fasted, the Holy Ghost said, Separate me Barnabas and Saul for the work whereunto I have called them. And when they had fasted and prayed, and laid their hands on them, they sent them away. So they, being sent forth by the Holy Ghost, departed unto Seleucia; and from thence they sailed to Cyprus. And when they were at Salamis, they preached the word of God in the synagogues of the Jews: and they had also John to their minister. Acts 13:2-5 (KJV)*

Notice that it was the Holy Spirit that called out Barnabas and Saul. It was not that they had a desire to be apostles and requested that they be put in that role, NO, the Holy Spirit called them. I believe we are too quick to put labels on people.

Many times you will find the most unlikely people are actually called and operating in these functions. It is not always the well-educated, The handsome or powerful that the Lord chooses. Paul tells us:

> *For [simply] consider your own call, brethren; not many [of you were considered to be] wise according to human estimates and standards, not many influential and powerful, not many of high and noble birth. [No] for God selected (deliberately chose) what in the world is foolish to put the wise to shame, and what the world calls weak to put the strong to shame. And God also selected (deliberately chose) what in the world is lowborn and insignificant and branded and treated with contempt, even the things that are nothing, that He might depose and bring to nothing the things that are, So that no mortal man should [have pretense for glorying and] boast in the presence of God. 1 Corinthians 1:26-29 Amplified*[10]

The first disciples were fishermen. I had heard that an apostle was coming to our fellowship and my immediate imagination was of a very powerful man of God. When he was introduced it was a bit of shock. Looking at him from a worldly perspective he was a small man, somewhat unkempt, with a very heavy southern accent. By all accounts you would completely overlook him if you saw him on the street. Yet he traveled all over the world and told some amazing stories of God's miraculous provision and protection. He spent time going from church to church laying in deacons and elders. As humans we look for the polished, highly educated professional, surely we think, this is who God would prefer for the work of the ministry. Even Samuel thought so in anointing the next King of Israel. 1 Samuel 16:6,7

> *When they arrived, Samuel saw Eliab, and said, "Surely he's the Lord's anointed." The Lord told Samuel, "Don't look at his appearance or his height, for I've rejected him. Truly, God does not see what man sees, for man looks at the outward appearance, but the Lord sees the heart."*

Paul did not have to call himself Apostle Paul, rather he said I am an Apostle indicating the function he was performing. All apostles prophesied, evangelized, shepherded and taught. The point to all these fourfold functions is that it is the function that is recognized not the title.

For there is one God, and one mediator between God and men, the man Christ Jesus; Who gave himself a ransom for all, to be testified in due time. Whereunto I am ordained a preacher, and an apostle, (I speak the truth in Christ, and lie not;) a teacher of the Gentiles in faith and verity. 1 Timothy 2:5-7

but now has been revealed by the appearing of our Savior Christ Jesus, who abolished death and brought life and immortality to light through the gospel, for which I was appointed a preacher and an apostle and a teacher. 2 Timothy 1:10,11 (NASB)

How do we know if someone is called to be a "sent one"? Paul says that the Apostle is both patient and manifests the miraculous. The life of an apostle is not an easy one filled with recognition and glory, to the contrary, it is generally filled with lack and suffering. It is critical that the one sent be called by the Lord, otherwise they will not be able to stand when the inevitable trouble comes upon them. Paul and Barnabas, in Acts 13, were set part by the Holy Spirit. This function should not be taken lightly because it will require a huge commitment on their part.

I am become a fool in glorying; ye have compelled me: for I ought to have been commended of you: for in nothing am I behind the very chiefest apostles, though I be nothing. Truly the signs of an apostle were wrought among you in all patience, in signs, and wonders, and mighty deeds. 2 Corinthians 12:11-12 (KJV)

Prophets

If we look at prophecy from a Jewish perspective we find that Prophecy is not prediction and fulfillment, prophecy is pattern. I heard Jacob Prasch explain it.

Take Hosea 11:1
When Israel was a child, then I loved him, and called my son out of Egypt.

The context is clearly speaking about Israel and not the Messiah but in Mathew 2:15 we have a reference to Yeshua that seems to be taken out of context by Matthew, unless you understand that prophecy is pattern.

> *And was there until the death of Herod: that it might be fulfilled which was spoken of the Lord by the prophet, saying, Out of Egypt have I called my son.*

What has been prophesied can be fulfilled repeatedly at different times. We see this in the abomination of desolation.

> *But when ye shall see the abomination of desolation, spoken of by Daniel the prophet, standing where it ought not, (let him that readeth understand,) then let them that be in Judaea flee to the mountains: Mar 13:14*

This phrase is applied in 1 Maccabees 1:57 to the altar to Zeus erected by Antiochus Epiphanes.

> On the fifteenth day of the month Casleu, in the hundred and forty-fifth year, king Antiochus set up the abominable idol of desolation upon the altar of God, and they built altars throughout all the cities of Juda round about:

If prophecy were prediction and fulfillment then according to the Maccabees, Daniel's prediction was already fulfilled. But Yeshua repeats the same thing long after Antiochus Epiphanes put the statue of Zeus in the Holy of Holies as something that is yet to come. What can we conclude from this? Remember, the Bible is a Jewish book, written by Jewish authors. Many false doctrines or beliefs result from not understanding the Hebrew mind set. Some will try to argue that the Book of Revelation has already been fulfilled. Others say that it is yet future. From a Jewish perspective they are both right because prophecy is not prediction and fulfillment, it is pattern. So the seven churches of Revelation chapters two and three were actual churches and they show us Church history in advance. It is a fascinating subject I would encourage you to research the subject in more depth.

The prophet speaks the word by revelation, they rebuke, make declarations, sometimes they condemn the actions of the believers to correct errors in belief and practice. These receive the word by revelation where teachers receive the word mostly by interpretation.

There are charismatic groups that are constantly proclaiming "thus saith the Lord" and most of it never comes to pass. In the Old Testament if someone made a declaration like that and it did not come to pass they were taken out and stoned. These modern day prophets are not held accountable for their mistakes. They unwittingly break the commandment which states "thou shall not take the name of the Lord in vain" By using the Lord's authority and declaring falsely that "the Lord says" they are walking on very unstable ground. It is especially galling to me to hear the TV evangelists say that "The Lord told me there are ten people watching right now who are to give $1000. I actually saw one guy repeat the same prediction year after year on the yearly telethon. Then there are those who predict that giving to their ministry will produce a blessing. There are real prophets today but there are far more false prophets preying on sincere believers who genuinely want to serve the Lord.

False prophets are those who foretell or speak correction in his Name and it does not come to pass… we have many false prophets who repeatedly make false prophecies today… If we say "thus saith the Lord" we better be sure it is He. If the Old Testament rules applied today we would see a lot less of them on TV.

A prophet then is not always someone who predicts the future but one who through divine revelation brings forth the Word of the Lord as it applies to a group or event now. It must aways agree with the written Word and must be 100% correct or they should be considered a false prophet. The prophet can provide guidance to the body.

Evangelists

> Strong's Number: g2099 Greek: euangelistes Evangelist: literally., "a messenger of good" (eu, "well," angelos, "a messenger"), denotes a "preacher of the Gospel," Act 21:8; Eph 4:11, which makes clear the distinctiveness of the function in the churches; 2Ti 4:5. Cp. euangelizo, "to proclaim glad tidings," and euangelion, "good news, gospel." Missionaries are "evangelists," as being essentially preachers of the Gospel. - Vines[9]

EK-KLĀ-SĒ'-Ä - Leadership

We have very little to go on when understanding what the evangelist does. The Evangelist is only mentioned three times. Even though Philip was originally chosen in the early church to minister to widows (Acts 6), he eventually becomes an "evangelist".

> *And the next day we that were of Paul's company departed, and came unto Caesarea: and we entered into the house of Philip the evangelist, which was one of the seven; and abode with him. Acts 21:8 (KJV)*

In 8:4–25, he evangelizes Samaria, and in 8:26–40, he leads the Ethiopian eunuch to salvation in Christ and baptizes him.

> *Therefore they that were scattered abroad went every where preaching the word. Then Philip went down to the city of Samaria, and preached Christ unto them. And the people with one accord gave heed unto those things which Philip spake, hearing and seeing the miracles which he did. For unclean spirits, crying with loud voice, came out of many that were possessed with them: and many taken with palsies, and that were lame, were healed. And there was great joy in that city. But there was a certain man, called Simon, which beforetime in the same city used sorcery, and bewitched the people of Samaria, giving out that himself was some great one: To whom they all gave heed, from the least to the greatest, saying, This man is the great power of God. And to him they had regard, because that of long time he had bewitched them with sorceries. But when they believed Philip preaching the things concerning the kingdom of God, and the name of Jesus Christ, they were baptized, both men and women. Then Simon himself believed also: and when he was baptized, he continued with Philip, and wondered, beholding the miracles and signs which were done. Acts 8:4-13 (KJV)*

> *And the angel of the Lord spake unto Philip, saying, Arise, and go toward the south unto the way that goeth down from Jerusalem unto Gaza, which is desert. And he arose and went: and, behold, a man of Ethiopia, an eunuch of great authority under Candace*

> queen of the Ethiopians, who had the charge of all her treasure, and had come to Jerusalem for to worship, Was returning, and sitting in his chariot read Esaias the prophet. Then the Spirit said unto Philip, Go near, and join thyself to this chariot. And Philip ran thither to him, and heard him read the prophet Esaias, and said, Understandest thou what thou readest? And he said, How can I, except some man should guide me? And he desired Philip that he would come up and sit with him. The place of the scripture which he read was this, He was led as a sheep to the slaughter; and like a lamb dumb before his shearer, so opened he not his mouth: In his humiliation his judgment was taken away: and who shall declare his generation? for his life is taken from the earth. And the eunuch answered Philip, and said, I pray thee, of whom speaketh the prophet this? of himself, or of some other man? Then Philip opened his mouth, and began at the same scripture, and preached unto him Jesus. Acts 8:26-35 (KJV)

Paul commissions Timothy with doing "the work of an evangelist"

> I charge thee therefore before God, and the Lord Jesus Christ, who shall judge the quick and the dead at his appearing and his kingdom; Preach the word; be instant in season, out of season; reprove, rebuke, exhort with all longsuffering and doctrine. For the time will come when they will not endure sound doctrine; but after their own lusts shall they heap to themselves teachers, having itching ears; And they shall turn away their ears from the truth, and shall be turned unto fables. But watch thou in all things, endure afflictions, do the work of an evangelist, make full proof of thy ministry. 2 Tim 4:1-5 (KJV)

It is also assumed by the apostolic fathers that the reader would understand what the work of an Evangelist was in those days.

> But surely if Luke, who always preached in company with Paul, and is called by him "the beloved," and with him performed the work of an evangelist, and was entrusted to hand down to us a Gospel, learned nothing different from him (Paul), as has been pointed out from his words, how can these men, who were never attached to Paul, boast that

they have learned hidden and unspeakable mysteries? Iranaeus - *Against Heresies: Book III* Chapter XIV.—*If Paul had known any mysteries unrevealed to the other apostles*

"the prophets have inquired and searched diligently," and what follows. It is declared by this that the prophets spake with wisdom, and that the Spirit of Christ was in them, according to the possession of Christ, and in subjection to Christ. For God works through archangels and kindred angels, who are called spirits of Christ. "Which are now," he says, "reported unto you by them that have preached the Gospel unto you." The old things which were done by the prophets and escape the observation of most, **_are now revealed to you by the evangelists._** "For to you," he says, "they are manifested by the Holy Ghost, who was sent;" that is the Paraclete, of whom the Lord said, If I go not away, He will not come. *Fragments of Clemens Alexandrinus*

The evangelist is very much like an apostle, traveling and preaching the good news of Yeshua and gathering the people together. In today's churches I have found that many of the Evangelists are very weak in the Word. In their enthusiastic delivery they put forth thoughts and ideas that are completely not Biblical. In some cases it is their outgoing charismatic personality that gets them invited to speak as an evangelist but their foundational doctrine is sorely lacking. Unlike Apostles who establish and maintain local fellowships and Prophets who bring an inspired Word for correction and direction the Evangelist brings forth the good news and inspires the local fellowship to do the work of evangelists in their communities. This is good as long as the Evangelist is solidly founded in the Word. In these days the Local Elders should be watchful and correct any derivation from the truth of the Word often found in today's evangelists.

Pastors (Shepherd)

The word is translated pastor in KJV only once in Ephesians. 4:11 everywhere else it is shepherd and has nothing to do with what we would call a pastor today. The function of a pastor is truly blown completely out of proportion to what the Word refers to as the Pastor and Teacher. The real New Testament "Pastors" shepherds are the Overseers (Elders).

Wuest word studies[5] - The words "pastors" and "teachers" are in a construction called Granvill Sharp's rule which indicates that they refer to one individual. The one who shepherds God's flock is also a teacher of the Word, having both the gifts of shepherding and teaching the flock. God's ideal pastor is one who engages in a didactic ministry, feeding the saints on expository preaching, giving them the rich food of the Word.

Strong's G4166. ποιμήν poimen; gen. poiménos, masc. noun. Shepherd, one who generally cares for flocks. Zodhiates[7]

"a shepherd, one who tends herds or flocks" (not merely one who feeds them "Pastors" guide as well as feed the flock; cp. Act 20:28, which, with Act 20:17, indicates that this was the service committed to elders (overseers or bishops); so also in 1Pe 5:1-2, "tend the flock ... exercising the oversight," RV; this involves tender care and vigilant superintendence. - Vines[9]

This word ποιμην is from a root meaning to protect. Jesus said the good shepherd lays down his life for the sheep (Joh 10:11) and called himself the Good Shepherd. In Heb 13:20 Christ is the Great Shepherd (cf. 1Pe 2:25). Only here are preachers termed shepherds (Latin pastores) in the N.T. But the verb ποιμαινω, to shepherd, is employed by Jesus to Peter (Joh 21:16), by Peter to other ministers (1Pe 5:2), by Paul to the elders (bishops) of Ephesus (Ac 20:28). Here Paul groups "shepherds and teachers" together. All these gifts can be found in one man, though not always. Some have only one. Robertson's Word Pictures[11]

Both Pastor and Teacher functions have different scopes but in the same person. A shepherd appeals to the will of the individual, while the teacher appeals more to one's intellect. It is the Elders in a local body who are the shepherds and teachers.

Teachers

Teachers receive the word mostly by interpretation where prophets receive the word by revelation. In order for a teacher to be truly effective they must have a thorough grasp on the entire word of God, they must understand that the entire Word of God was written down by Jews. The Bible is a very Jewish book. It cannot be completely understood without knowing how the Jews understand it otherwise somethings will not make sense. This is where misinterpretation and false doctrine come into the church. We have already discussed one aspect of this where prophecy is pattern. Not understanding that can lead to misunderstanding and misinterpretation.

Teachers: Strong's Number G1320 matches the Greek διδάσκαλος (didaskalos), which occurs 58 times in 57 verses in the Greek concordance of the KJV

Teach: The KJV translates Strongs G1321 in the following manner: teach (93x), taught (with G2258) (4x). usage for didaskalos is to denote teachers within the church. Acts 13:1 states,

> *Now there were in the church that was at Antioch certain prophets and teachers; as Barnabas, and Simeon that was called Niger, and Lucius of Cyrene, and Manaen, which had been brought up with Herod the tetrarch, and Saul.*

Both 1 Corinthians 12:28- 29 and Ephesians 4:11 list "teachers" as gifts to the church. We are warned by James that teachers have a grave responsibility to teach truth.

> *My brethren, be not many masters (G1321), knowing that we shall receive the greater condemnation. James 3:1*

Paul also describes himself as a didaskalos:

> *Whereunto I am ordained a preacher, and an apostle, (I speak the truth in Christ, and lie not;) a teacher of the Gentiles in faith and verity. 1 Timothy 2:7*

> *Whereunto I am ordained a preacher, and an apostle, (I speak the truth in Christ, and lie not;) a teacher of the Gentiles in faith and verity. 2 Timothy 1:11*

Keep in mind that there are only two offices in the church: Elder/Overseer/Bishop and Deacon. The four functions: Apostle, Prophet, Evangelist,

EK-KLĀ-SĒ'-Ä - Leadership

Pastor/teacher are functions for the body at large. These may have a local fellowship as a home base but are generally not in the local body all the time. I do not see where a "pastor" is a single individual. It is the Elders (plural) who do the local shepherding,teaching and governing and the Deacons serve the physical needs of the local fellowship.

I am diametrically opposed to TV preachers and evangelists because they do not come under the leadership of the local fellowship. They can say whatever they want true or false without consequences. I believe this to be a very dangerous practice. Yes, there are many good teachers out there and on the Internet. Christians have, for so long, been starved of the true meat of the Word. Churches have failed in their mission to equip the saints to do the work of the ministry, feeding them instead a diet of milk and not meat so they have never matured. These sheep are potential targets for false teachers and false prophets. Wake up! It is time to return to New Testament Christianity especially as we see the day approaching.

1 - New King James Bible - Thomas Nelson Publishers
2 - International Standard Bible -
3 - Dr. Bob Utley - Bible Lessons International - http://www.freebiblecommentary.org/
4 - Expositors Bible Commentary - Zondervan
5 - Word Studies from the Greek New Testament - Kenneth S. Wuest - William B. Eerdmans Publishing Company
6 - Thayer's Greek-English Lexicon of the New Testament - Joseph Thayer - Hendrickson Publishers
7 - Complete Word Study Dictionary - Dr. Spiros Zodhiates - AMG Publishers
8 - Mounce's Complete Expository Dictionary of Old and New Testament Words - William D. Mounce - Zondervan
9 - Vine's Complete Expository Dictionary of Old and New Testament Words - W.E. Vine and Merrill F. Unger - Thomas Nelson
10 - Amplified Bible - Zondervan
11 - Word Pictures in the New Testament - A.T. Robertson - Broadman Press

The Church History of Eusebius.
And again after mentioning other matters, they say:

"For, through the genuineness of their love, their greatest contest with him was that the Beast, being choked, might cast out alive those whom he supposed he had swallowed. For they did not boast over the fallen, but helped them in their need with those things in which they themselves abounded, having the compassion of a mother, and shedding many tears on their account before the Father.

They asked for life, and he gave it to them, and they shared it with their neighbors. Victorious over everything, they departed to God. Having always loved peace, and having commended peace to us they went in peace to God, leaving no sorrow to their mother, nor division or strife to the brethren, but joy and peace and concord and love."

This record of the affection of those blessed ones toward the brethren that had fallen may be profitably added on account of the inhuman and unmerciful disposition of those who, after these events, acted unsparingly toward the members of Christ.

Chapter II.—The Martyrs, beloved of God, kindly ministered unto those who fell in the Persecution.
- *The Church History of Eusebius.*

4

Operation of the ekklāsē'ä

We have some insight into how the early church operated from the New Testament epistles. These epistles generally corrected errors in practice or warn against heresy. Some clues come from the writing of the early church fathers. We must keep in mind that our only true guide can be the scriptures anything that contradicts that should be considered false. Even in the very early church Satan was there to bring in deception and heresy, so we must be careful in listening to these writings and judge it against scripture. We have some indication in Acts:

> *And they continued stedfastly in the apostles' doctrine and fellowship, and in breaking of bread, and in prayers. And fear came upon every soul: and many wonders and signs were done by the apostles. And all that believed were together, and had all things common; And sold their possessions and goods, and parted them to all men, as every man had need. And they, continuing daily with one accord in the temple, and breaking bread from house to house, did eat their meat with gladness and singleness of heart, Praising God, and having favour with all the people. And the Lord added to the church daily such as should be saved. Acts 2:42-47 (KJV)*

We start with the most crucial part of any New Testament fellowship without this, we should close our doors and go home, without this nothing else matters; it is love. But not just any type of love, agape love. Of the four Greek words for love this is the one most needed in our fellowships today.

Agape Love

> *A new commandment I give unto you, That ye love one another; as I have loved you, that ye also love one another. By this shall all men know that ye are my disciples, if ye have love one to another. John 13:34-35 (KJV)*

Do the brothers and sisters love one another? A fellowship's health is determined by their love for one another. James 3 tells us *"For where envying and strife is, there is confusion and every evil work"*. We know that 1 Corinthians 13 is the love chapter, however, it is critical that we combine it with the last paragraph of chapter 12 as a prequel to that chapter. Paul is talking about the operation of the ek-klā-sē'-ä but then turns and describes what true agape love is. It was true in his day as it is in our day. We can all get caught up in daily operations and forget that the greatest part of Christianity is our love for one another. The world will not recognize us because we have great buildings, magnificent worship or stirring sermons. No! Yeshua told us they would recognize us for our love for one another.

> *Now ye are the body of Christ, and members in particular. And God hath set some in the church, first apostles, secondarily prophets, thirdly teachers, after that miracles, then gifts of healings, helps, governments, diversities of tongues. Are all apostles? are all prophets? are all teachers? are all workers of miracles? Have all the gifts of healing? do all speak with tongues? do all interpret? But covet earnestly the best gifts: and yet shew I unto you a more excellent way.*
>
> *Though I speak with the tongues of men and of angels, and have not charity, I am become as sounding brass, or a tinkling cymbal. And though I have the gift of prophecy, and understand all mysteries, and all knowledge; and though I have all faith, so that I could remove mountains, and have not charity, I am nothing. And though I bestow all my goods to feed the poor, and though I give my body to be burned, and have not charity, it profiteth me nothing. Charity suffereth long, and is kind; charity envieth not; charity vaunteth not itself, is not puffed up, Doth not behave itself unseemly, seeketh not her own, is not easily provoked, thinketh no evil; Rejoiceth not in iniquity, but rejoiceth in the truth; Beareth all things, believeth all things, hopeth all things, endureth all things.*
> 1 Corinthians 12:27- 13:1-7 (KJV)

Tertullian writing in the second century emphasized the kind of love the early Christians had for each other.

> It is mainly the deeds of a love so noble that lead many to put a brand upon us. **"See," they say, "how they love one another,"** for they themselves are animated by mutual hatred. "How they are ready even to die for one another!" For they themselves will sooner put to

> death.... we are regarded as having less claim to be held true brothers, that no tragedy causes trouble in our brotherhood, [and] the family possessions, which generally destroy brotherhood among you, create fraternal bonds among us. One in mind and soul, we do not hesitate to share our earthly goods with one another. All things are common among us but our wives. - Tertullian, c. A.D. 200 Apology 39

We, who are in the body of Christ and in our fellowships should be more aware of other's needs. We were in Florida working at a Christian school barely scraping by. One day Cindy drove our only car to school. After she was getting her class started, someone came running in and screamed your car is on fire! Some oil had leaked on to the engine and started the fire. There was nothing to be done, it was totaled. Then some nice Christian man came walking by and casually said "Well it is only a car," as he got into his new car and drove off. I am not suggesting that he should have given her his car but the attitude with too many of us is: "O well, I am glad that is not my problem. I will pray for you". This was not the way in the early church. They had all things in common. We know in Acts that they even sold their possessions to share with the ek-klā-sē'-ä. Recall the story of Ananias and Sapphira in Acts 5. William Ramsay gives us some insight.

> ...general instructions were issued that members of the Church ought to distribute to the poor all that they possessed. But many of the owners of property (" as many as were possessors of lands or houses'), of their own free will, from love of the brethren, used from time to time to sell their property and bring the proceeds to the Apostles. They acquired merit and honour by these acts of self-sacrifice; and two examples are given, one honest and meritorious, one dishonest and disgraceful (Ananias and Sapphira).
>
> Sir William Mitchell Ramsay[1], 1851-1939.
> *Pictures of the apostolic church, its life and thought*

The issue with Ananias and Sapphira was that they were going to receive merit and honor dishonorably through deceit. By implying that they had sold the property and held nothing back was a lie. Peter knew this through the power of the Holy Spirit. I am not sure why we don't see the same thing happening in our fellowships today. We may be able to fool the people but not the Holy Spirit.

What did Yeshua say about giving?

> *Give to every man that asketh of thee; and of him that taketh away thy goods ask them not again. And as ye would that men should do to you, do ye also to them likewise. Luke 6:30-31 (KJV)*

The church we were attending decided to have a "revival" meeting. Personally I don't believe you can "plan to have a revival" That is totally up to the Holy Spirit and happens at His direction and certainly without planning. Paul even said:

> *Who then is Paul, and who is Apollos, but ministers by whom ye believed, even as the Lord gave to every man? I have planted, Apollos watered; but God gave the increase. So then neither is he that planteth any thing, neither he that watereth; but God that giveth the increase. Now he that planteth and he that watereth are one: and every man shall receive his own reward according to his own labour. 1 Corinthians 3:5-8 (KJV)*

I asked those in leadership why they wanted to have a meeting like that. I don't remember the response but I asked what they had done in the community that would give the right to ask people to come? Had they fed the poor and hungry, had they helped the widows and orphans in their need? What love had they shown the community? I knew with the exception of a handful of people, they had been completely inwardly focused. The day arrived but the people did not. If you want to be loved you must first love others. Zig Ziglar used to say "No one cares how much you know until they know how much you care". It is essential that today we should show genuine love and care for others.

> *Pure religion and undefiled before God and the Father is this, To visit the fatherless and widows in their affliction, and to keep himself unspotted from the world. James 1:27 (KJV)*

I highly recommend Nancy Missler's book and audio series, *"the Way of Agape"* Available from www.kingshighway.org. Here are a couple of excerpts.

> Agape is God's "supernatural" Love and it's the only solid basis upon which a relationship can be built. Only upon this foundation can all the human loves be built, rebuilt and allowed to grow. One of the reasons why so many relationships are falling apart today is because God's Agape Love is missing. God's Love is missing because the people involved are either unbelievers or they have quenched God's Love in their hearts with bitterness, resentment, or unforgiveness and are not willing to give these things over to God.
>
> The verb that is used for love in these two commandments is "agapao." To agapao God means to continually seek to obey, trust, and follow God's Will and not our own. In other words, we are to continually yield our own thoughts, emotions, and desires that are contrary to His and choose to worship and serve Him only. Loving God is not an emotional feeling. It's not an emotional high. Loving God is losing self to the point where we can say, "there was not a 'me' (self) there," only God. This is the point where we will know Jesus is not just in our lives, He is our Life.
> Nancy Missler - *The Way of Agape*[2]
>
> By love have all the elect of God been made perfect; without love nothing is well-pleasing to God.
> Clement of Rome -*The First Epistle of Clement to the Corinthians* chapter 49

On the opposite side of the coin is what we should not love: the world and the things in the world. This is what causes us to become cold to the Lord. When we begin to fear; loss of jobs, loss of material things and money, loss of health, or just generally being fearful, this is a clear indicator that your love for the Lord has grown cold. John tells us that there is no fear in perfect love.

Herein is our love made perfect, that we may have boldness in the day of judgment: because as he is, so are we in this world. There is no fear in love; but perfect love casteth out fear: because fear hath torment. He that feareth is not made perfect in love. We love him, because he first loved us. If a man say, I love God, and hateth his brother, he is a liar: for he that loveth not his brother whom he hath seen, how can he love God whom he hath not seen? And this commandment have we from him, That he who loveth God love his brother also. 1 John 4:17-21 (KJV)

We get a glimpse of this perfect love from the The Martyrdom of Ignatius. Ignatius was sentenced to die by wild beasts. Yet he is not fearful but rejoices in the Lord.

> Then Trajan pronounced sentence as follows: "We command that Ignatius, who affirms that he carries about within him Him that was crucified, be bound by soldiers, and carried to the great [city] Rome, there to be devoured by the beasts, for the gratification of the people." When the holy martyr heard this sentence, he cried out with joy, "I thank thee, O Lord, that Thou hast vouchsafed to honour me with a perfect love towards Thee, and hast made me to be bound with iron chains, like Thy Apostle Paul." Having spoken thus, he then, with delight, clasped the chains about him; and when he had first prayed for the Church, and commended it with tears to the Lord, he was hurried away by the savage cruelty of the soldiers, like a distinguished ram the leader of a goodly flock, that he might be carried to Rome, there to furnish food to the bloodthirsty beasts.
> *The Martyrdom of Ignatius* - Ante-Nicene Fathers Volume 1

Love not the world, neither the things that are in the world. If any man love the world, the love of the Father is not in him. For all that is in the world, the lust of the flesh, and the lust of the eyes, and the pride of life, is not of the Father, but is of the world. And the world passeth away, and the lust thereof: but he that doeth the will of God abideth for ever. 1 John 2:15-17 (KJV)

We are admonished not to fear persecution and death by Tertullian.

> He who fears to suffer, cannot belong to Him who suffered. But the man who does not fear to suffer, he will be perfect in love—in the love, it is meant, of God; "for perfect love casteth out fear." "And therefore many are called, but few chosen." It is not asked who is ready to follow the broad way, but who the narrow. And therefore the Comforter is requisite, who guides into all truth, and animates to all endurance. And they who have received Him will neither stoop to flee from persecution nor to buy it off, for they have the Lord Himself, One who will stand by us to aid us in suffering, as well as to be our mouth when we are put to the question.
> *De Fuga in Persecutione* 208AD by Tertullian

Teaching

"teaching," which in Greek is didaché (dē-dä-khā - doctrine)

C.H. Dodd said there was three forms of teaching in the early church:

> The New Testament writers draw a clear distinction between preaching and teaching. The distinction is preserved alike in Gospels, Acts, Epistles, and Apocalypse, and must be considered characteristic of early Christian usage in general. Teaching (didaskein) is in a large majority of cases ethical instruction. Occasionally it seems to include what we should call apologetic, that is, the reasoned commendation of Christianity to persons interested but not yet convinced. Sometimes, especially in the Johannine writings, it includes the exposition of theological doctrine. Preaching, on the other hand, is the public proclamation of Christianity to the non-Christian world. The verb keryssein properly means "to proclaim." A keryx may be a town crier, an auctioneer, a herald, or anyone who lifts up his voice and claims public attention to some definite thing he has to announce. Much of our preaching in Church at the present day would not have been recognized by the early Christians as kerygma. It is teaching, or exhortation (paraklesis), or it is what they

called homilia, that is, the more or less informal discussion of various aspects of Christian life and thought, addressed to a congregation already established in the faith.
The Apostolic Preaching and Its Developments - C.H. Dodd[3]

Jacob Prasch gives a good analogy of this by describing this trinity of teaching with a tripod. With only one leg and the thing topples over, two legs and the things is more stable but can not stand on its own. But with three legs the thing is stable and can stand on its own. This would apply to the church as well as individuals. There are churches which are very evangelical, but lack the other two. There are fellowships which are very good in doctrine and exhortation but have no outreach. It is clear that we must have all three if we are to have a stable and living organism call the ek-klā-sē'-ä .

I have seen this my entire life in many churches. I was raised in a Baptist church were virtually every sermon was directed at evangelism. This makes for a very weak Christian. This does not equip the saints to go out and do the work of evangelism. Nor does it equip the saint to stand against the wiles of the enemy. We must have all three to have a balanced fellowship which equips the saints to face the world and come into maturity. I have seen Christians believe a lot of silly things simply because they do not know the foundational truths of the Word. In these days of apostasy we must teach our people the foundational truths and the whole Word of God. There will come a time when it is a lot more difficult to learn the truth. The following describes the three legs.

1. **Kerygma - Evangelical** - The aim was to show the need for repentance and regeneration. Without an outreach to the lost, the fellowship becomes stale, introverted and eventually dead. This is sorely lacking in many of today's Charismatic churches.

2. **Homilia - Exhortation** (paraklesis (para, "beside," kaleo, "to call"), or it is what they called homilia, to call the members to live the teachings and commandments of the Lord. This is almost non-existent in today's seeker friendly churches because it calls the member to live a separate life wholly unto the Lord. This would not sit well with those who want to feel that have met the requirements of some obligation but do not want their lives interrupted by it.

It is essential that we call people to holy living. Without it, the wolves can easily come in and devour the flock. The word becomes compromised by giving into changes in the culture. Eventually, left unchecked, the fellowship will slip into sin because they become unequally yoked with the world. Look what happen to Solomon, the wisest man in the world, by being yoked with pagan wives, he eventually fell and God's judgment came against him. We should learn from his mistake.

> *But King Solomon loved many strange women, together with the daughter of Pharaoh, women of the Moabites, Ammonites, Edomites, Zidonians, and Hittites; Of the nations concerning which the Lord said unto the children of Israel, Ye shall not go in to them, neither shall they come in unto you: for surely they will turn away your heart after their gods: Solomon clave unto these in love. And he had seven hundred wives, princesses, and three hundred concubines: and his wives turned away his heart. For it came to pass, when Solomon was old, that his wives turned away his heart after other gods: and his heart was not perfect with the Lord his God, as was the heart of David his father. For Solomon went after Ashtoreth the goddess of the Zidonians, and after Milcom the abomination of the Ammonites. And Solomon did evil in the sight of the Lord, and went not fully after the Lord, as did David his father. Then did Solomon build an high place for Chemosh, the abomination of Moab, in the hill that is before Jerusalem, and for Molech, the abomination of the children of Ammon. And likewise did he for all his strange wives, which burnt incense and sacrificed unto their gods. And the Lord was angry with Solomon, because his heart was turned from the Lord God of Israel, which had appeared unto him twice, And had commanded him concerning this thing, that he should not go after other gods: but he kept not that which the Lord commanded. Wherefore the Lord said unto Solomon, Forasmuch as this is done of thee, and thou hast not kept my covenant and my statutes, which I have commanded thee, I will surely rend the kingdom from thee, and will give it to thy servant. 1 Kings 11:1-11 (KJV)*

3. Didsakein - Doctrine - foundational truths. The basic doctrine of the Word is not being taught today in a general sense. Do people know why they believe what the believe or do they just accept what they are told?

Can the normal member talk to a Jew or a Jehovah Witness and tell them why Yeshua is the Messiah or why Jesus is God who came in the flesh? These are just a few of the important foundational truths. Hosea makes a valid point, we will be destroyed because we don't have the knowledge or understanding of the Word.

> *My people are destroyed for lack of knowledge: because thou hast rejected knowledge, I will also reject thee, that thou shalt be no priest to me: seeing thou hast forgotten the law of thy God, I will also forget thy children. Hosea 4:6*

Ordinances: Baptism and The Lord's Supper

There are two ordinances of the New Testament Church; Baptism and The Lord's Supper. It is necessary that you understand that John's baptism and Christian baptism are not the same. In Acts we are told to baptize in the name of the Yeshua, this is to distinguish between the Old Testament baptism of repentance unto God done by John and the baptism which identifies us with the death, burial and resurrection of our Lord. In Matthew the Lord told us to baptize in three names:

> *Go ye therefore, and teach all nations, baptizing them in the name of the Father, and of the Son, and of the Holy Ghost: Matthew 28:19*

Those that say we should only baptize in Yeshua's name confuse John's baptism with Christian baptism.

Baptism

The Jews have a form of baptism called the Mik'vot. This baptism was performed by women after their minstrel cycle to become ritually clean. In a Jewish marriage there is also a ceremony which requires the woman to do a Mik'va. The priest's in the Old Testament had requirements of ceremonial washing before entering into service. I believe this is why Yeshua was baptized by John not for repentance.

EK-KLĀ-SĒ'-Ä - Operation

> *And Aaron and his sons thou shalt bring unto the door of the tabernacle of the congregation, and shalt wash them with water. Exodus 29:4 (KJV)*

> *And the Lord spake unto Moses, saying, Take the Levites from among the children of Israel, and cleanse them. And thus shalt thou do unto them, to cleanse them: Sprinkle water of purifying upon them, and let them shave all their flesh, and let them wash their clothes, and so make themselves clean. Numbers 8:5-7 (KJV)*

In a general sense John's baptism was one of repentance unto God. Today's baptism is identification with the Messiah in His death, burial and resurrection.

> The Idea of Baptism. It was solemnly instituted by Christ, shortly before his ascension, to be performed in the name of the Father, the Son, and the Holy Spirit. **It took the place of circumcision as a sign and seal of church membership.** It is the outward mark of Christian discipleship, the rite of initiation into the covenant of grace. It is the sacrament of repentance (conversion), of remission of sins, and of regeneration by the power of the Holy Spirit. *History of the Christian Church, Volume I: Apostolic Christianity. A.D. 1-100* Schaff, Philip

What is the purpose of baptism? To be perfectly clear, baptism ***does not*** save you. Some teach that baptism is a requirement to be saved. But that would mean the thief on the cross next to Yeshua is in hell. Yeshua did not say that. Baptism is an outward acknowledgment of an internal truth. You are identifying yourself with the Messiah's death, burial and resurrection. It makes sense that the early apostolic fathers would see it as a replacement for circumcision. Circumcision was an outward sign of a Jew being a servant of the most holy God. But that did not save them either. However, the only word we have from scripture is:

> *For he is not a Jew, which is one outwardly; neither is that circumcision, which is outward in the flesh: But he is a Jew, which is one inwardly; and **circumcision is that of the heart**, in the*

spirit, and not in the letter; whose praise is not of men, but of God. Romans 2:28-29 (KJV)

Infant baptism is foolishness. An infant can not identify with the Messiah, what He did in his death burial and resurrection. They can not repent or be born-again. I do believe that if an infant dies before they have the ability to reason and accept the Messiah, that they automatically are taken by the Lord. The fallacy of the belief is that some are told that if they are baptized as an infant they are saved, this is a very dangerous lie. Church membership and infant baptism do not grant salvation! Remember, Yeshua said that "narrow is the way and there are few who find it".

During the reformation, those who did not teach infant baptism were called Anabaptists. Anabaptist New Latin anabaptista, "one who is rebaptized," from Late Greek anabaptizein, "to baptize again." What is not normally taught is that the Anabaptists were persecuted by both the Catholic as well as the Protestant churches for their beliefs. I believe it will happen again.

The following is an excerpt for the website
http://www.anabaptists.org/history/what-is-an-anabaptist.html

> The differences between the Anabaptists and the Magisterial Reformers lay much deeper than any outward sign, including that of baptism. **The Anabaptists were earnestly concerned with the restitution of the true church on an Apostolic model. The Anabaptists considered the state churches beyond reformation.**
>
> The era of the 16th-century Protestant Reformation in Europe spawned a number of radical reform groups, among them the Anabaptists. These Christians regarded the Bible as their only rule for faith and life. Because of their radical beliefs, the Anabaptists were persecuted by Protestants as well as by Roman Catholics.
>
> The evangelical and non-revolutionary Anabaptists of Switzerland, Austria, Germany, and the Netherlands, were a

trial to the leading reformers because of their radical views on the nature of the church and of the Christian ethic.

There is no single defining set of beliefs, doctrines, and practices that characterizes all Anabaptists.

Contemporary groups with early Anabaptist roots include the Mennonites, Amish, Dunkards, Landmark Baptists, Hutterites, and various Beachy and Brethren groups.

Anabaptists have been characterized historically by a love for the Word of God, and by a strict demand for holiness of life.

Baptism of the Holy Spirit

Do you get the Holy Spirit when you are born-again? Yes of course! What is the baptism of the Holy Spirit? You receive the Holy Spirit at regeneration. Yeshua breathed on the disciples and they received the Holy Spirit. This was after His resurrection and before the Outpouring of the Spirit in Acts chapter 2.

Receiving the Spirit at new birth

> *Then said Jesus to them again, Peace be unto you: as my Father hath sent me, even so send I you. And when he had said this, he breathed on them, and saith unto them,* **Receive ye the Holy Ghost**: *John 20:21-22 (KJV)*

> *In the last day, that great day of the feast, Jesus stood and cried, saying, If any man thirst, let him come unto me, and drink. He that believeth on me, as the scripture hath said, out of his belly shall flow rivers of living water. (***But this spake he of the Spirit, which they that believe on him should receive: for the Holy Ghost was not yet given; because that Jesus was not yet glorified.***) John 7:37-39*

For those just being born-again on the day of Pentecost **_received_** the Holy Spirit.

> *Then Peter said unto them, Repent, and be baptized every one of you in the name of Jesus Christ for the remission of sins, and ye*

*shall **receive the gift** of the Holy Ghost. Acts 2:38 (KJV)*

The gentiles in Samaria had accepted the Word and were water baptized but the Spirit had not come to them yet.

Now when the apostles which were at Jerusalem heard that Samaria had received the word of God, they sent unto them Peter and John: Who, when they were come down, prayed for them, that they might receive the Holy Ghost: (For as yet he was fallen upon none of them: only they were baptized in the name of the Lord Jesus.) Then laid they their hands on them, and they received the Holy Ghost. Acts 8:14-17 (KJV)

By the Holy Spirit we become a part of one body.

*For by o**ne Spirit are we all baptized into one body**, whether we be Jews or Gentiles, whether we be bond or free; and have been all made to drink into one Spirit. For the body is not one member, but many. 1 Corinthians 12:13-14 (KJV)*

The Gentiles believed and the evidence to the Jewish believers that they had received the Holy Spirit was speaking in tongues.

*While Peter yet spake these words, the Holy Ghost fell on all them which heard the word. And they of the circumcision **which believed** were astonished, as many as came with Peter, because that on the **Gentiles also was poured out the gift of the Holy Ghost**. For they heard them speak with tongues, and magnify God. Then answered Peter, Can any man forbid water, that these should not be baptized, which have received the Holy Ghost as well as we? And he commanded them to be baptized in the name of the Lord. Then prayed they him to tarry certain days. Acts 10:44-48 (KJV)*

Being filled with the Spirit

There is a difference between receiving the Holy Spirit and being filled. First, look at the terminology used: "filled with the Spirit".

*And they were all **filled** with the Holy Ghost, and began to speak with other tongues, as the Spirit gave them utterance. Acts 2:4*

*See then that ye walk circumspectly, not as fools, but as wise, Redeeming the time, because the days are evil. Wherefore be ye not unwise, but understanding what the will of the Lord is. And be not drunk with wine, wherein is excess; but **be filled with the Spirit**; Speaking to yourselves in psalms and hymns and spiritual songs, singing and making melody in your heart to the Lord; Giving thanks always for all things unto God and the Father in the name of our Lord Jesus Christ; Ephesians 5:15-20 (KJV)*

*Then Peter, **filled with the Holy Ghost**, said unto them, Ye rulers of the people, and elders of Israel, Acts 4:8 (KJV)*

For John truly baptized with water; but ye shall be baptized with the Holy Ghost not many days hence. Acts 1:5 (cf Acts 16:11)

In this case the word is baptized which literally means overwhelmed or completely immersed. The disciples were certainly immersed on the day of Pentecost. Receiving the Holy Spirit is a one time event that happens at new birth. Being filled with the Spirit happens over and over again. It cannot be said that you get the Holy Spirit at birth and then you have a second infilling of the Spirit on a ***one-time*** time basis as some Pentecostals and Charismatics teach. The Greek tenses in Ephesians 5:18 give us the answer. Be filled is the verb πληρόω Pleroo it is in imperative mode meaning that it is, of course, an imperative action that we be filled and it is in the present tense meaning it is a continual action in the now. The important point is that it is a passive verb meaning that the subject is acted on. This is not some type of action that we do to work ourselves into a "spiritual frenzy". It is the work of the Holy Spirit. We see in many of the recent so called revivals people being worked up to the point where they are out of control. This is not the Holy Spirit. No where in the fruits of the Spirit do we find that kind of foolishness. When you see people out of control run to the nearest exit, it is either a work of Satanic influence or foolishness on the part of the participant.

The Lord's Supper

I heard recently that someone was claiming that the Last Supper was not a Passover meal that they ate regular bread. I was quite disturbed about that because I had just finished a book which described how the Last Supper was a perfect antitype of the Old Testament Passover type and shadow. This person claimed that since the Last Supper was eaten before the 14th of Nissan (The beginning of the Passover Feast) they ate regular bread. He supports his theory on the fact that the Greek word for bread there is often used to indicate regular bread. I did not want to rely on my own bias concerning the Passover so I went to a man who is both Jewish and a Christian. Since I don't have his permission to use his name here, I will not mention who it is. This man is very learned in both Greek and Hebrew and speaks both fluently. He is well trained in both Jewish and Christian history. Here is his take on the subject of the last supper and the use of the Greek word for bread.

> I do know that the Greek term for bread is 'artos' and could mean any kind of bread either leavened or matzah (MT. 26:26, MK. 14:22, LK. 22:19, 1 Cor. 11:23). Artos (case ending variation 'arton') is used for unleavened bread / matzah in The Septuagint in Leviticus 8: 2,26). "Klao" however means to crack or break bread. It has no meaning at all as to if or not the bread was leavened. There is no linguistic support for these conclusions whatsoever in Greek or in Hebrew. None at all. In Ex. 12: 1-28 The Paschal Seder regulation required unleavened bread which is what Jesus used at The Last Supper.

We must remember that the Bible is a Jewish book. Yeshua asked the early disciples, who were Jewish, to go and prepare the Passover.

> *And the disciples did as Jesus had appointed them; and they made ready the **passover**. Matt 26:19 (KJV)*

For Yeshua to eat leavened bread at a Passover meal would be a sin, it would destroy the type and shadow set forth in Exodus.

> *And they shall take of the blood, and strike it on the two side posts and on the upper door post of the houses, wherein they shall eat it. And they shall eat the flesh in that night, roast with fire, and **unleavened bread;** and with bitter herbs they shall eat it. Ex 12:7-8 (KJV)*

He told the disciples that He had a desire to eat the Passover meal before he suffered. Not a new kind of meal called the Last Supper.

> *And when the hour was come, he sat down, and the twelve apostles with him. And he said unto them, With desire I have desired to eat this passover with you before I suffer:*
> Luke 22:14-15 (KJV)

Matt 26:23-30 - I believe that the Passover meal or Last Supper follows the typical Passover Seder as commanded in Exodus. I have inserted the various parts of the Seder which correspond to the last supper. For more detail you can get my book *"Dayenu - A Christian view of Passover with the Haggadah"*.[4] It is available on Amazon or email me at haggadah@worldsofwonderpublishing.com if you can not afford to buy it, I will send you a copy for any donation.

> *"And he answered and said, He that dippeth his hand with me in the dish* **[Step 4 Karpas]**, *the same shall betray me. The Son of man goeth as it is written of him: but woe unto that man by whom the Son of man is betrayed! it had been good for that man if he had not been born. Then Judas, which betrayed him, answered and said, Master, is it I? He said unto him, Thou hast said. And as they were eating,* **[Step 11 Shulchan Orech – the meal]** *Jesus took bread [matzot], and blessed it, and brake it* **[step 12 Eat the Afikoman]** *, and gave it to the disciples, and said, Take, eat; this is my body. And he took the cup, and gave thanks* **[step 13 the 3rd cup - Barech]**, *and gave it to them, saying, Drink ye all of it; For this is my blood of the new testament, which is shed for many for the remission of sins. But I say unto you, I will not drink henceforth of this fruit of the vine, until that day when I drink it new with you in my Father's kingdom. And when they had sung an hymn,* **[step 14 Hallel without drinking the 4th cup]** *they went out into the mount of Olives."*

In an article by Dr. Arnold Fruchtenbaum[5] there are three views of the Last Supper.

1. **Transubstantiation** - The Catholics believe that the bread and wine actually becomes the body and blood of the Messiah. Not Biblical.

2. **Consubstantiation** - The Lutherans believe that the bread and the wine actually contain the elements of the Messiah. Not Biblical.

3. **A memorial** - *For as often as ye eat this bread, and drink this cup, ye do* **shew the Lord's death till he come**. 1 Corinthians 11:26 (KJV)

> The "breaking of bread," so often alluded to by Luke, is undoubtedly an act of religion. It is an accompaniment of the meal in the house : the bread was broken and divided to all as a symbol that all were parts of one whole, one fellowship, one Church, one Master. The common meal was thus a bond of union among the brotherhood, and the young Church aimed at encouraging this union in every way—amongst others, by carrying charity to such a pitch that they regarded their property as common, and people used to sell their possessions and divide them to all according to their varying needs.
> Sir William Mitchell Ramsay - *Pictures of the apostolic church, its life and thought*[1]

Gifts of the Spirit

The gifts of the Spirit are widely misunderstood by the body. The word translated gifts is actually from the root Strong's G5485 - charis χάρις which is where we get the word grace. The word gifts is not in the original. A better translation would be powers or manifestations.

> *For by grace* G5485 *are ye saved through faith; and that not of yourselves: it is the gift* G1435 *of God: - Eph 2:8*

The word gift Strong's G1435 is actually dōron δῶρον a gift or present. If that were the word in 1 Corinthians 12 for the gifts of the Spirit it would mean something entirely different. It would be a present that we receive. The word used in 1 Corinthians 12 is G5486 - charisma χάρισμα a gift of divine grace. We are told in verse 11: *"But all these worketh that one and the selfsame Spirit, dividing to every man severally as he will"*. You may have the grace to operate in any one of the manifestations of the Spirit since He distributes to whom ever He wills! Whatever ministry God has called you to may require one or many of these manifestations of grace at any point in time. That does not mean that you have been given a present of any one of these manifestations that you can use all of the time. I think this is where the trouble comes in. I hear people say I have the gift of healing. That may be true from time to time as it is needed for building up the body of Christ. Lets examine what Paul says:

> *Now there are diversities of gifts, but the same Spirit. And there are differences of administrations, but the same Lord. And there are diversities of operations, but it is the same God which worketh all in all. But the manifestation of the Spirit is given to every man to profit withal. For to one is given by the Spirit the word of wisdom; to another the word of knowledge by the same Spirit; To another faith by the same Spirit; to another the gifts of healing by the same Spirit; To another the working of miracles; to another prophecy; to another discerning of spirits; to another divers kinds of tongues; to another the interpretation of tongues: But all these worketh that one and the selfsame Spirit, dividing to every man severally as he will. 1 Corinthians 12:4-11*

It is the Holy Spirit who decides what is manifested if it is a true manifestation, there are fake and fabricated manifestations. What is the end purpose of these manifestations? The building up and edification of the body of believers. The first test we must make in judging a manifestation is does it build up the body or edify? If it does neither then it can be questioned.

> *Even so ye, forasmuch as ye are zealous of spiritual [gifts], seek that ye may excel to the edifying of the church. Wherefore let him that speaketh in an unknown tongue pray that he may interpret. For if I pray in an unknown tongue, my spirit prayeth, but my understanding is unfruitful. 1 Corinthians 14:12-14 (KJV)*

The early church taught that the gifts would be fully in operation until the Second Coming. However, there are those who would have us believe that the gifts of the Spirit ceased when the Bible canon was complete quoting Paul in Corinthians.

> *Charity never faileth: but whether there be prophecies, they shall fail; whether there be tongues, they shall cease; whether there be*

knowledge, it shall vanish away. For we know in part, and we prophesy in part. But when that which is perfect is come, then that which is in part shall be done away.
1 Corinthians 13:8-10 (KJV)

To use that as an excuse to say that the gifts (manifestations), more specifically the gift of tongues, has ceased is ludicrous. First Paul would have had no way of knowing that his letters would be put in a book we call the Bible. Second, knowledge would have to vanish. Irenaeus in the forth book of *Against Heresies* is very clear about what that which is perfect means; It is the second coming of Jesus:

> He bestows more and greater [gifts]; as also the Lord said to His disciples: "Ye shall see greater things than these." And Paul declares: "Not that I have already attained, or that I am justified, or already have been made perfect. For we know in part, and we prophesy in part; but when that which is perfect has come, the things which are in part shall be done away." As, therefore, **when that which is perfect is come, we shall not see another Father, but Him whom we now desire to see** (for "blessed are the pure in heart: for they shall see God"); neither shall we look for another Christ and Son of God, but Him who [was born] of the Virgin Mary, who also suffered, in whom too we trust, and whom we love;

Others will say that the gifts stopped when the twelve apostles all died. This idea does not hold with the truth. I thoroughly believe that the gifts still exist today. However, there are serious abuses and fabrications.

We see in today's meetings false teachers, false prophets and false manifestations. This is not the first time this has happened. The early church fathers talk about false gifts even in the early days of Christianity. According to the writings of the apostolic fathers, the gifts are to be in operation until the Second Coming. But even in the early days, Satan was there sowing seeds of doubt by filling some with his own false manifestations. It is understandable why many fellowships today want to ban spiritual manifestations in the services. In many cases they have seen abuses and false manifestations of the true Spirit of God. Often these so called manifestations are fabricated by the person themselves or through the power of demons.

I was in one meeting where we were asked if we had a need to come up for prayer. The young man who was praying for me began to push on my forehead, I resisted, he then pushed harder in a effort to have me "fall out in the Spirit", but if I went down it would not be because of the Spirit it would have been because he pushed me off balance. This type of show is why many churches do not allow the Holy Spirit to come in and I understand. This is charlatanism at its worst!

There are many prophecy groups claiming to have the Word of the Lord. Yet most of their predictions do not come to pass. I can give you many examples especially when they put a time frame on its fulfillment. One man prophesied that in the fall of 2013 Christians would experience great abundance. Unfortunately none of us, including the man who made the prediction experienced abundance, in fact, it was just the opposite. This makes him a false prophet. Jacob Prasch tells about going to a Taro Card Reader before he became a Christian. She predicted that he would become a follower of Jesus. Even the wicked can be right some of the time. But in the Old Testament if a prophet made a prediction that did not come true he was stoned to death as a false prophet. We must be very careful not to take the name of the Lord in vain by saying, "thus says the Lord" when it is not the Lord, but wishful thinking.

On one hand, we have fellowships that refuse entrance to the Holy Spirit in their meetings. On the other hand, we have those claiming that the Holy Spirit has moved in a meeting with false manifestations where He has not. We dare not fabricate a gift and claim that it was the Holy Spirit. This is equally as wrong, if not more so, than denying Him altogether.

On the other side of the issue, I have seen true gifts where tongues were spoken and then interpreted by someone in the meeting and a person who spoke that language confirmed what was said. It is critical that what is said be judged by those in authority. In the last days we know that the enemy will be doing false miracles and manifesting false gifts. In these days there is a growing infatuation for the supernatural. **DO NOT** believe everything you see or hear because Satan has the ability to counterfeit miracles. These false miracles will increase in these end times. Remember what Paul told Timothy about the miracles that Jannes and Jambres did replicating the Miracles of God through Moses in Egypt (see Targum of Jonathan on Ex 7:11):

> *Now as Jannes and Jambres withstood Moses, so do these also resist the truth: men of corrupt minds, reprobate concerning the faith. 2Timothy 3:8*

Justin Martyr speaks about Simon and Menander and how they deceived the early Christians with magic and false miracles:

> But the evil spirits were not satisfied with saying, before Christ's appearance, that those who were said to be sons of Jupiter were born of him; but after He had appeared, and been born among men, and when they learned how He had been foretold by the prophets, and knew that He should be believed on and looked for by every nation, they again, as was said above, put forward other men, the Samaritans Simon and Menander, who did many mighty works by magic, and deceived many, and still keep them deceived. For even among yourselves, as we said before, Simon was in the royal city Rome in the reign of Claudius Cæsar, and so greatly astonished the sacred senate and people of the Romans, that he was considered a god, and honoured, like the others whom you honour as gods, with a statue.
> Justin Martyr - *The First Apology Chapter 56 —The demons still mislead men.*

Prophecy

Remember that to the Jew prophecy is pattern. It is not necessarily prediction and a one time fulfillment example:

> *And when they were departed, behold, the angel of the Lord appeareth to Joseph in a dream, saying, Arise, and take the young child and his mother, and flee into Egypt, and be thou there until*

> *I bring thee word: for Herod will seek the young child to destroy him. 14 When he arose, he took the young child and his mother by night, and departed into Egypt: And was there until the death of Herod: that it might be fulfilled which was spoken of the Lord by the prophet, saying, Out of Egypt have I called my son.*
> Matt 2:13-15 (KJV) (see Hosea 11:1)

Jacob Prasch[6] explains the idea of prophecy being pattern like this: Abraham was called by God back out of Egypt, Israel was called back out of Egypt by God during the Exodus, Joseph, Mary and Jesus were called out of Egypt according to Matthew 2, Christians are called out of the world (Egypt being the type)in 1 Corinthians 10, Finally, in Revelation we will be taken out of Egypt at the Rapture.

There will not be any new doctrine as a result of someone prophesying. If there are those who say that there is a new belief, be very aware. Generally speaking the false prophet will mix truth with error. That is why it is critical that any fellowship have mature solid leadership to oversee the flock and to correct error.

> *Beware of false prophets, which come to you in sheep's clothing, but inwardly they are ravening wolves. Ye shall know them by their fruits. Do men gather grapes of thorns, or figs of thistles? Even so every good tree bringeth forth good fruit; but a corrupt tree bringeth forth evil fruit. A good tree cannot bring forth evil fruit, neither can a corrupt tree bring forth good fruit. Every tree that bringeth not forth good fruit is hewn down, and cast into the fire. Wherefore by their fruits ye shall know them. Matthew 7:15-20 (KJV)*

> Strong's G4396 προφήτης one who, moved by the Spirit of God and hence his organ or spokesman, solemnly declares to men what he has received by inspiration, especially concerning future events, and in particular such as relate to the cause and kingdom of God and to human salvation Brown, Driver, Briggs[7]

> *But the prophet, which shall presume to speak a word in my name, which I have not commanded him to speak, or that shall speak in*

> the name of other gods, even that prophet shall die. and if thou say in thine heart, How shall we know the word which the Lord hath not spoken? When a prophet speaketh in the name of the Lord, if the thing follow not, nor come to pass, that is the thing which the Lord hath not spoken, but the prophet hath spoken it presumptuously: thou shalt not be afraid of him. Deut 18:20-22

> *Dialogue with Trypho Chapter LXXXII.—*
> *The prophetical gifts of the Jews were transferred to the Christians.* "For the prophetical gifts remain with us, even to the present time.
> **Justin Martyr** 110-165AD

Speaking in tongues

> **Ireaneaus - Book Six** *Against Heresies*
> Now the soul and the spirit are certainly a part of the man, but certainly not the man; for the perfect man consists in the commingling and the union of the soul receiving the spirit of the Father, and the admixture of that fleshly nature which was molded after the image of God. For this reason does the apostle declare, "We speak wisdom among them that are perfect," terming those persons "perfect" who have received the Spirit of God, and who through the Spirit of God do speak in all languages, as he used Himself also to speak. In like manner we do also hear many brethren in the Church, who possess prophetic gifts, and who through the Spirit speak all kinds of languages, and bring to light for the general benefit the hidden things of men, and declare the mysteries of God, whom also the apostle terms "spiritual," they being spiritual because they partake of the Spirit, and not because their flesh has been stripped off and taken away, and because they have become purely spiritual.

The manifestation of tongues is valid for today just as it was in the first century. I have seen two types of tongues. The first is what Paul refers to in 1 Corinthians in the nine gifts where someone speaks in a tongue and another interprets. This I believe to be a known tongue like that which the people heard in Acts chapter two. If there is someone in your fellowship who can understand the language you speak when speaking by the Spirit then Paul would accept your speaking in the fellowship. There are some whose manifestation is that of a known human tongue. Then, the second type is used strictly as a prayer language. Sometimes, we don't know what to pray, it is then that speaking in tongues becomes very necessary.

> *For if I pray in an unknown tongue, my spirit prayeth, but my understanding is unfruitful. What is it then? I will pray with the spirit, and I will pray with the understanding also: I will sing with the spirit, and I will sing with the understanding also.*
> 1 Corinthians 14:14-15 (KJV)

Raising the dead

Even after the apostles, the local body was raising the dead. I know that this is still possible today. I have to admit that we prayed for two hours for a man to come back, but he did not. There is a ministry here in Dallas that has seen the dead raised several times. In one instance the woman did not come back to life. When they inquired of the husband it turned out that the couple had made an agreement that they would not try to bring each other back. However, the man was lonely and went against the agreement. Evidently the woman decided to stay where she was.

The Simon referred to in the following quotes is Simon Magus. We first learn about him in Acts 8 where he tries to buy the ability to lay hands on people and have them receive the Holy Spirit.

> In the treatise, *Against Heresies,* a work now generally ascribed to Hippolytus, bishop of Portus, near Rome, about A.D. 218-235, we find a general outline of the principles of Simon Magus and his school. Some account also is given in the same treatise of the Great Announcement, a writing compiled from the oral teaching of Simon, by one of his immediate followers: in this compilation the revelation with which he declared he was entrusted is set forth, and the work and Person of Christ are disparaged and set aside. Simon is by many regarded as the father of Gnosticism.
> Phillip Schaff - *Commentary on the New Testament*

Moreover, those also will be thus confuted who belong to Simon and Carpocrates, and if there be any others who are said to perform miracles—who do not perform what they do either through the power of God, or in connection with the truth, nor for the well-being of men, but for the sake of destroying and misleading mankind, by means of magical deceptions, and with universal deceit, thus entailing greater harm than good on those who believe them, with respect to the point on which they lead them astray. For they can neither confer sight on the blind, nor hearing on the deaf, nor chase away all sorts of demons—[none, indeed,] except those that are sent into others by themselves, if they can even do so much as this. Nor can they cure the weak, or the lame, or the paralytic, or those who are distressed in any other part of the body, as has often been done in regard to bodily infirmity. Nor can they furnish effective remedies for those external accidents which may occur. **And so far are they from being able to raise the dead, as the Lord raised them, and the apostles did by means of prayer, and as has been frequently done in the brotherhood on account of some necessity—the entire Church in that particular locality entreating [the boon] with much fasting and prayer, the spirit of the dead man has returned, and he has been bestowed in answer to the prayers of the saints**—that they do not even believe this can be possibly be done, [and hold] that the resurrection from the dead is simply an acquaintance with that truth which they proclaim.
Irenaeus AD 177 - *Against Heresies - Book 2 Chapter 31*

There may be cases where for various reasons a person can be brought back from a state of separation from the body. We have seen via video a man in Africa who had been dead for three days. This man had even been embalmed. His wife never gave up but took his stiff body to a meeting that was being held in the village and he came back from the dead. I do not have first hand knowledge of this event but I still believe it happened.

Demons

We have an overabundance of evidence that there are demons in the world today. There are also principalities and powers of darkness. I do not believe that a Christian can be possessed by a demon but they can have influence in our lives. The early church was in the habit of driving evil spirits out of people. However, I can not find one reference where a Christian was held captive by a demon. But we must remember that we wrestle not against flesh and blood but against principalities and powers in the air. There is real deliverance and there are fake ones. In recent years there has been an over emphasis on deliverance. In many cases we have a situation where it is mostly fabricated. An easy way to tell if you are under the influence of a power other than the Holy Spirit, or your flesh for that matter, is to check your fruit as Paul describes it in Galatians. You can have the fruit of walking in the flesh or you can have the fruit of walking in the Spirit. It is your choice which to follow. Paul names almost two to one the works of the flesh.

> *This I say then, Walk in the Spirit, and ye shall not fulfil the lust of the flesh. For the flesh lusteth against the Spirit, and the Spirit against the flesh: and these are contrary the one to the other: so that ye cannot do the things that ye would. But if ye be led of the Spirit, ye are not under the law. Now the works of the flesh are manifest, which are these;*
>
> *Adultery, fornication, uncleanness, lasciviousness, Idolatry, witchcraft, hatred, variance, emulations, wrath, strife, seditions, heresies, Envyings, murders, drunkenness, revellings, and such like: of the which I tell you before, as I have also told you in time past, that they which do such things shall not inherit the kingdom of God.*
>
> *But the fruit of the Spirit is **love**, **joy**, **peace**, **longsuffering**, **gentleness**, **goodness**, **faith**, **Meekness**, **temperance**: against such there is no law.*
> Galatians 5:16-23 (KJV)

> For some certainly and truly drive out devils, so that those who have thus been cleansed from evil spirits frequently both believe [in Christ], and join themselves to the Church.

Others have foreknowledge of things to come: they see visions, and utter prophetic expressions. Others still, heal the sick by laying their hands upon them, and they are made whole. Yea, moreover, as I have said, the dead even have been raised up, and remained among us for many years. And what shall I more say? It is not possible to name the number of the gifts which the Church, [scattered] throughout the whole world, has received from God, in the name of Jesus Christ, who was crucified under Pontius Pilate, and which she exerts day by day for the benefit of the Gentiles, neither practicing deception upon any, nor taking any reward from them [on account of such miraculous interpositions]. For as she has received freely from God, freely also does she minister [to others]. Irenaeus AD 177 *Heresies Book 2* Chapter 32—*Further exposure of the wicked and blasphemous doctrines*

One of the worst things Christians can do is to drive out demons from an unsaved person who is not willing to accept the Messiah as their savior. The possibility exists that this demon will come round again finding his former home clean can invite more of his fellow demons to join him back in his former room making the situation even worse than before.

Are demons the offspring of fallen Angels?

I have thought for some time now that demons are not fallen angels. One reason is that demons have a desperate need to inhabit a body. Angels have a body and are capable of physical manifestation in human like form. Demons are never spoken of as having a body of their own. If they are the offspring of fallen angels they would not have a human soul and could never be saved like the true human race. When they spoke to Yeshua it was always "have you come to destroy us before the time?" They evidently understand that there is no salvation for them and at some point in the future they will be punished. We know that Satan has a hierarchy and demons are most likely at the bottom. Justin Martyr indicates that they are the offspring of fallen Angels, I have no reason to doubt him. Although he may have read about that in the book of Jubilees. We can only guess right now based on the Word in Genesis where we read about the Nefilium.

> But the angels transgressed this appointment, and were captivated by love of women, and begat children who

are those that are called demons; and besides, they afterwards subdued the human race to themselves, partly by magical writings, and partly by fears and the punishments they occasioned, and partly by teaching them to offer sacrifices, and incense, and libations, of which things they stood in need after they were enslaved by lustful passions; and among men they sowed murders, wars, adulteries, intemperate deeds, and all wickedness. Whence also the poets and mythologists, not knowing that it was the angels and those demons who had been begotten by them that did these things to men, and women, and cities, and nations.
The Second Apology of Justin for the Christians Addressed to the Roman Senate - Justin Martyr - Chapter 5

When Almighty God, to beautify the nature of the world, willed that that earth should be visited by angels, when they were sent down they despised His laws. Such was the beauty of women, that it turned them aside; so that, being contaminated, they could not return to heaven. Rebels from God, they uttered words against Him. Then the Highest uttered His judgment against them; and from their seed giants are said to have been born. By them arts were made known in the earth, and they taught the dyeing of wool, and everything which is done; and to them, when they died, men erected images. But the Almighty, because they were of an evil seed, did not approve that, when dead, they should be brought back from death. Whence wandering they now subvert many bodies, and it is such as these especially that ye this day worship and pray to as gods.
Instructions of Commodianus Commodianus 240AD. Chapter 3—*The Worship of Demons.*

There is a world which cannot be seen with human eyes. It is the realm of demons and angels. Remember the story of Elisha and his servant:

And Elisha prayed, and said, Lord, I pray thee, open his eyes, that he may see. And the Lord opened the eyes of the young man; and he saw: and, behold, the mountain was full of horses and chariots of fire round about Elisha - 2 Kings 6:17 (KJV)

If we could see into the domain of the spirit we would be shocked at what we would find. The principalities and the powers that surround us as well as God's angels there to protect us. I would guess that it would be too distracting. There is a reason that God designed us to hear only somewhere between ~12 Hz to 20k Hz. We can smell between 4,000 and 10,000 smells. Our eyesight is limited as well. We can detect about 10 million different colors but can not see radio waves. There are millions of radio waves all around us from cell phones, radio stations and even the Internet. If we could see all of this information we would be overwhelmed. God knows what we need and designed us in a specific way. A lot of things will open up when we get our glorified bodies.

Worship

Praise although extremely necessary is not Worship. In most churches the worship service has become a concert. It is a time of entertainment. We attended one very large church in Dallas where they hired professional musicians so the music would be good enough for broadcast TV. This church eventually failed and the city took over the property.

In the late sixties and early seventies at the beginning of the Christian rock era the music was very evangelistic. Most of the music was aimed at telling people about Jesus and why you need Him. Here are just a very few; Larry Norman - *I wish we had all been ready,* Keith Green's - *How can they live without Jesus,* Second Chapter of Acts - *Now that I belong to you,* Children of the Day - *For those tears I died and New life,* Sweet Comfort Band - *Somebody Loves you,* The Way - *You're Caught in a world,* Talbot Brothers - *I hear you callin'* there are many more. There was a very wide variety of musical styles, heavy rock to folk music. In churches people were beginning to sing the scripture and psalms.

Then a major shift came in the mid-seventies and music became "big business". Since that time (in a general sense) the music has become self-centered; What will God do for me. It is more about entertainment than glorifying God. I was in a Christian store and the radio station was playing contemporary Christian music. Every song sounded the same. The same instruments, the same beat so much so that I could not tell the difference between songs. When the songs were softer or slower every vocalist was "breathy" and maudlin. Is this Holy Spirit inspired or fabricated? If you have a chance listen to music from the late sixties early seventies and compare it to today and make up your own mind. The early contemporary Christian music may not always be slick and professionally produced but had incredible impact by the power of the Holy Spirit. As a Christian I can not listen to the music being produced today and I am sure the world has no time for it either...

Many years ago as I was seeking the Lord I believe that the Holy Spirit revealed that Psalm 95 was a pattern for entering into worship.

> *O come, let us sing unto the Lord: let us make a joyful noise to the rock of our salvation. Let us come before his presence with thanksgiving, and make a joyful noise unto him with psalms. For the Lord is a great God, and a great King above all gods. In his hand are the deep places of the earth: the strength of the hills is his also. The sea is his, and he made it: and his hands formed the dry land. O come, let us worship and bow down: let us kneel before the Lord our maker. For he is our God; and we are the people of his pasture, and the sheep of his hand. To day if ye will hear his voice, Harden not your heart, as in the provocation, and as in the day of temptation in the wilderness: When your fathers tempted me, proved me, and saw my work. Forty years long was I grieved with this generation, and said, It is a people that do err in their heart, and they have not known my ways: Unto whom I sware in my wrath that they should not enter into my rest. Psalms 95:1-11 (KJV)*

What the church calls worship is many times just praise. Please do not get me wrong there is great benefit in praise and thanksgiving to the Lord. Here, however, we are talking about worship. I hear people say "wasn't that a great worship service", speaking about the emotion they felt by the moving of sensual music. But, worship is not about singing worship songs, it far more than that.

If we analyze Psalm 95 we discover something interesting. In the beginning there is singing and thanksgiving. This is followed by a sense of awe about God's greatness. Then something happens that causes the worshiper to bow down and acknowledge that we are His people, the sheep of His pasture. We get a sense of belonging to the Lord. At this point we have understood who God is, what He has done and what we are to Him. Then there is an odd shift in the Psalm to a warning. The Psalm states that if we hear His voice we should not harden our hearts as the Israelites did in the desert.

It is clear that God wants to fellowship with us. He wants us to seek Him and when we do He will speak to us. I hear some say that God does not speak to us today, that everything He needed to say is in the Bible. I agree in a general sense and if what we are hearing is contrary to the Word we need to be very cautious and seek further confirmation. Remember Peter and the unclean animals.

> *On the morrow, as they went on their journey, and drew nigh unto the city, Peter went up upon the housetop to pray about the sixth hour: And he became very hungry, and would have eaten: but while they made ready, he fell into a trance, And saw heaven opened, and a certain vessel descending unto him, as it had been a great sheet knit at the four corners, and let down to the earth: Wherein were all manner of four footed beasts of the earth, and wild beasts, and creeping things, and fowls of the air. And there came a voice to him, Rise, Peter; kill, and eat. But Peter said, Not so, Lord; for I have never eaten any thing that is common or unclean. And the voice spake unto him again the second time, What God hath cleansed, that call not thou common. This was done thrice: and the vessel was received up again into heaven. Now while Peter doubted in himself what this vision which he had seen should mean, behold, the men which were sent from Cornelius had made inquiry for Simon's house, and stood before the gate, And called, and asked whether Simon, which was surnamed Peter, were lodged there. While Peter thought on the vision, the Spirit said unto him, Behold, three men seek thee. Arise therefore, and get thee down, and go with them, doubting nothing: for I have sent them. Acts 10:9-20*

What may not be obvious to us Gentiles is that the Jews were told to have nothing to do with Gentiles. Because of the context I do not think that the vision was necessarily about eating unclean animals but everything to do with associating with unclean Gentiles. While he was in the vision the Lord told Peter to go with the three men at the door. This would be an example of God asking Peter to go against what he had been taught.

I have first hand experience that God does speak to us as individuals, giving direction and insight that would not be found in His Word. I was hired before I finished college by Texas Instruments in Dallas Texas. After graduation, my wife Cindy and I moved to Dallas. We knew no one in the area. Texas Instruments gave us enough money for 30 days to find a place to live. After searching diligently for a few weeks, the Lord told Cindy that we would talk to a man who had a house. He would give us one price and then lower it. This is exactly what happened. This is just one very small example of the many examples we could give. Yes, the Lord does speak to us today. That bit of information would never have been found in the Word, it is too personal and too timely.

The Word reminds us in many places the blessings of seeking the Lord. We have already mentioned King Asa in the introduction.

> *The angel of the Lord encampeth round about them that fear him, and delivereth them. O taste and see that the Lord is good: blessed is the man that trusteth in him. O fear the Lord, ye his saints: for there is no want to them that fear him. The young lions do lack, and suffer hunger: but they that seek the Lord shall not want any good thing. Psalms 34:7-10 (KJV)*

There is no want to them that fear Him and they that seek the Lord will not want any good thing.

What was the problem in Psalm 95? Paul tells us, it was unbelief:

> *Wherefore (as the Holy Ghost saith, Today if ye will hear his voice, Harden not your hearts, as in the provocation, in the day of temptation in the wilderness: When your fathers tempted me, proved me, and saw my works forty years. Wherefore I was grieved with that generation, and said, They do alway err in their heart; and they have not known my ways. So I sware in my wrath, They*

> shall not enter into my rest.) Take heed, brethren, lest there be in any of you an evil heart of unbelief, in departing from the living God. But exhort one another daily, while it is called To day; lest any of you be hardened through the deceitfulness of sin. For we are made partakers of Christ, if we hold the beginning of our confidence steadfast unto the end; While it is said, To day if ye will hear his voice, harden not your hearts, as in the provocation. For some, when they had heard, did provoke: howbeit not all that came out of Egypt by Moses. But with whom was he grieved forty years? was it not with them that had sinned, whose carcases fell in the wilderness? And to whom sware he that they should not enter into his rest, but to them that believed not? So we see that they could not enter in because of unbelief. Hebrews 3:7-19 (KJV)

Worship is about a moment by moment trusting relationship with a living God not a once or twice a week song service. You can worship a lot of things without singing songs to it; money, career, girlfriend and the list is endless. We worship God when we seek Him, put our trust in Him and obey Him.

> Take heed, then, often to come together to give thanks to God, and show forth His praise. For when ye come frequently together in the same place, the powers of Satan are destroyed, and his "fiery darts" urging to sin fall back ineffectual. For your concord and harmonious faith prove his destruction, and the torment of his assistants. Nothing is better than that peace which is according to Christ, by which all war, both of aërial and terrestrial spirits, is brought to an end. "For we wrestle not against blood and flesh, but against principalities and powers, and against the rulers of the darkness of this world, against spiritual wickedness in heavenly places."
> Ignatius (a disciple of John) - *Epistle to the Ephesians*

Healing

Here is an enigma. Some people are physically healed other are not. Why? Only God knows. Does God heal today? Yes, I have seen it first hand! My wife and son were carrying a 4x8 sheet of plywood. My son drop his end which made my wife drop hers on the top of her foot. You could see the bone sticking up under the skin. My son prayed for healing and the bone popped back in place. She went to work the next and taught school. I personally had a brain tumor on the pituitary gland. After many prayed a word came that the Lord would dissolve the tumor. This is exactly what happen. The doctors said that there was a brown liquid that came out but nothing that could be biopsied.

Most Christians quote Isiah 53:

> *But he was wounded for our transgressions, he was bruised for our iniquities: the chastisement of our peace was upon him; and with his stripes we are healed.* Isaiah 53:5 (KJV)

There are a couple of ways to view this text. One, by his taking the stripes we are physically healed. This is the way most people interpret this verse. Two, he healed our sin nature by taking on our punishment. I tend to lean to the second interpretation. Because God's word is always true, we can trust it without hesitation. God can not lie so if that meant physical healing anyone accepting his sacrifice on their behalf would always be healed. That may involve physical healing. But since we do not see this consistently there must be another explanation. Many times having your sins forgiven does result in a physical healing.

> *And, behold, they brought to him a man sick of the palsy, lying on a bed: and Jesus seeing their faith said unto the sick of the palsy; Son, be of good cheer; thy sins be forgiven thee. And, behold, certain of the scribes said within themselves, This man blasphemeth. And Jesus knowing their thoughts said, Wherefore think ye evil in your hearts? For whether is easier, to say, Thy sins be forgiven thee; or to say, Arise, and walk? But that ye may know that the Son of man hath power on earth to forgive sins, (then saith he to the sick of the palsy,) Arise, take up thy bed, and go unto thine house.*
> Matthew 9:2-6

> *Erastus abode at Corinth: but Trophimus have I left at Miletum sick.* 1 Timothy 4:20

If anyone would know about healing it would be Paul. But in 1 Timothy we learn that he left Trophimus at Miletum sick. We know that God heals instantly and other times he heals over time. There are times where using doctors is the right thing to do. We can not be stubborn and say that God only heals by casting out demons or by just having "enough faith". We know of people who died in "faith" refusing medical attention.

It is very much like the story of a man who was caught in a flood and had to get to the top of his house to survive. He prayed that God would rescue him. A man came in a row boat and asked it he needed help. The man refused because he was waiting for God to answer him. Sadly the Lord did answer him, but he had a different expectation so he refused. How many times do we set an expectation and if it does not come exactly as we had thought, we reject the Lords answer.

If we examine how Yeshua healed various people. It was not always the same. We can expect that the Lord heals his way not by a canned set of prayers or techniques. I am suspicious of anyone who says they have the "prayers" that will heal the sick. It is the Lord who heals not a set of rules or techniques.

Scriptures used by most faith healers:[13]

Physical or Spiritual Healing?
Surely he hath borne our griefs, and carried our sorrows: yet we did esteem him stricken, smitten of God, and afflicted. But he was wounded for our transgressions, he was bruised for our iniquities: the chastisement of our peace was upon him; and **with his stripes we are healed**. *Isaiah 53:4-5 (KJV)*

[12]Healed: Strong's H7495. rāpa': can mean physical and spiritual healing

Who did no sin, neither was guile found in his mouth: Who, when he was reviled, reviled not again; when he suffered, he threatened not; but committed himself to him that judgeth righteously: Who his own self bare our sins in his own body on the tree, that we, being dead to sins, should live unto righteousness: **by whose stripes ye were healed.** *For ye were as sheep going astray; but are now returned unto the Shepherd and Bishop of your souls.*
1 Peter 2:22-25 (KJV)

healed: **ē-ä'-o-mī** [11] - figuratively, of spiritual "healing,"

[12] Metaphorically, of moral diseases, to heal or save from the consequences of sin (Matt. 13:15; John 12:40; Acts 28:27 Heb. 12:13; James 5:16; 1 Pet. 2:24;

That it might be fulfilled which was spoken by Isaiah the prophet, saying, Himself took our infirmities, and bare our sicknesses. Matthew 8:17

[12] *Strong's3554. nósos; Metaphorically, pain, sorrow, evil (Matt. 8:17 from Is. 53:4)*

Is it possible that his stripes healed our sin nature and not our physical bodies? You will have to make up your own mind.

Healing by casting out demons

In some cases the Lord healed people by casting out demons. That does not mean however that every sickness is a demon. We see a lot of church services where that is all that they do.

When the even was come, they brought unto him many that were possessed with devils: and he cast out the spirits with his word, and healed all that were sick: That it might be fulfilled which was spoken by Isaiah the prophet, saying, Himself took our infirmities, and bare our sicknesses. Matthew 8:16,17

And in the synagogue there was a man, which had a spirit of an unclean devil, and cried out with a loud voice, Saying, Let us alone; what have we to do with thee, thou Jesus of Nazareth? art thou come to destroy us? I know thee who thou art; the Holy One of God. And Jesus rebuked him, saying, Hold thy peace, and come out of him. And when the devil had thrown him in the midst, he came out of him, and hurt him not. And they were all amazed, and spake among themselves, saying, What a word is this! for with authority and power he commandeth the unclean spirits, and they come out. And the fame of him went out into every place of the country round about.

Jesus Heals Many And he arose out of the synagogue, and entered into Simon's house. And Simon's wife's mother was taken with a great fever; and they besought him for her. And he stood over her, and rebuked the fever; and it left her: and immediately she arose and ministered unto them. Now when the sun was setting, all they that had any sick with divers diseases brought them unto him; and he laid his hands on every one of them, and healed them. And devils also came out of many, crying out, and saying, Thou art Christ the Son of God. And he rebuking them suffered them not to speak: for they knew that he was Christ. Luke 4:33-41

They shall take up serpents; and if they drink any deadly thing, it shall not hurt them; they shall lay hands on the sick, and they shall recover. Mark 16:18 (KJV)

Ask, and it shall be given you; seek, and ye shall find; knock, and it shall be opened unto you:
Matt 7:7 (KJV)

Verily I say unto you, Whatsoever ye shall bind on earth shall be bound in heaven: and whatsoever ye shall loose on earth shall be loosed in heaven. 19 Again I say unto you, That if two of you shall agree on earth as touching any thing that they shall ask, it shall be done for them of my Father which is in heaven. 20 For where two or three are gathered together in my name, there am I in the midst of them. Matt 18:18-20 (KJV)

Confession

A friend, Wendell Wright, recently pointed out a practice which has been lost to the church found in James 5:19 where James tells us:

Confess your faults one to another, and pray one for another, that ye may be healed. The effectual fervent prayer of a righteous man availeth much. James 5:16 (KJV)

There are many practices that were done in the early church which are not a part of the church today. This is mainly due to the fact that people have distorted and ignored what the scriptures tell us. People are quick to quote the first part of this paragraph but ignore the rest. The entire paragraph reads:

> *Is anyone among you afflicted (ill-treated, suffering evil)? He should pray. Is anyone glad at heart? He should sing praise [to God]. Is anyone among you sick? He should call in the church elders (the spiritual guides). And they should pray over him, anointing him with oil in the Lord's name. And the prayer [that is] of faith will save him who is sick, and the Lord will restore him; and if he has committed sins, he will be forgiven. Confess to one another therefore your faults (your slips, your false steps, your offenses, your sins) and pray [also] for one another, that you may be healed and restored [to a spiritual tone of mind and heart]. The earnest (heartfelt, continued) prayer of a righteous man makes tremendous power available [dynamic in its working].*
> James 5:13-16 - Amplified Bible[8]

Where did the practice of confession to a priest originate? Certainly after Constantine became a so called "Christian" error rapidly entered the ekklāsē'ä. Listen to how St. Augustine and St. Ambrose take the power to forgive sin as a function of the church.

> St. Augustine warns the faithful: "**Let us not listen to those who deny that the Church of God has power to forgive all sins**"[10] (De agon. Christ., iii).

> St. Ambrose
> rebukes the Novatianists who "professed to show reverence for the Lord by reserving to Him alone the power of forgiving sins. Greater wrong could not be done than what they do in seeking to rescind His commands and fling back the office He bestowed. . . . The Church obeys Him in both respects, by binding sin and by loosing it; for the Lord willed that for both the power should be equal"[10] (De poenit., I, ii,6)

> "This (forgiving sins), you say, only God can do. Quite true: but what He does through His priests is the doing of His own power"[10] (Ep. I ad Sympron, 6 in P.L., XIII, 1057)

Here is why, scripturally, the idea of confessing to a priest to get forgiveness is incorrect.

1. We are all priests

1 Peter 2:5 *Ye also, as lively stones, are built up a spiritual house, an holy priesthood, to offer up spiritual sacrifices, acceptable to God by Jesus Christ.*

*Rev. 1:6 *And hath made us kings and priests unto God and his Father; to him be glory and dominion for ever and ever. Amen.*

*Rev. 5:10 *And hast made us unto our God kings and priests: and we shall reign on the earth.*

* the King James Version incorrectly translates this verse. It should read *"a kingdom of priests"* as Wuest[9] does: *"who constituted us a kingdom, priests to His God and Father"*

2. We can come to the throne ourselves

Heb. 4:15-16 *For we have not an high priest which cannot be touched with the feeling of our infirmities; but was in all points tempted like as we are, yet without sin. Let us therefore come boldly unto the throne of grace, that we may obtain mercy, and find grace to help in time of need.*

3. There is only one mediator between man and God

1 Tim. 2:5 *For there is one God, and one mediator between God and men, the man Christ Jesus;*

4. No mention of confessing to a priest

1 John 1:9 *If we confess our sins, he is faithful and just to forgive us our sins, and to cleanse us from all unrighteousness.*

James 5:14-16 *Is any sick among you? let him call for the elders of the church; and let them pray over him, anointing him with oil in the name of the Lord: and the prayer of faith shall save the sick, and the Lord shall raise him up; and if he have committed sins, they shall be forgiven him. Confess your faults one to another, and pray one for another, that ye may be healed. The effectual fervent prayer of a righteous man availeth much.*

5. Incorrect assumptions

John 20:22-23 *And when he had said this, he breathed on them, and saith unto them, Receive ye the Holy Ghost: Whose soever sins ye remit, they are remitted unto them; and whose soever sins ye retain, they are retained.*

The Catholics believe that this verse gave the apostles the authority to forgive sin and that authority is passed down to their priest. I see no scriptural basis for that belief. Additionally there is no mention of confession here. They also use Matthew 16:18,19 (binding and loosing) as the basis for their for the church's authority to forgive sins.

And I say also unto thee, That thou art Peter, and upon this rock I will build my church; and the gates of hell shall not prevail against it. And I will give unto thee the keys of the kingdom of heaven: and whatsoever thou shalt bind on earth shall be bound in heaven: and whatsoever thou shalt loose on earth shall be loosed in heaven

The Catholics claim that Peter was the first Pope. But there is no historical or biblical evidence for that belief. We have already stated that there are only two offices in the New Testament church; Elder and Deacon. But, as always when bureaucrats get involved you get many layers of control. This practice of confessing to a priest is not scriptural! Here is are a quotes from the Didache, written around 70 AD.

At the church meeting you must confess your sins, and not approach prayer with a bad conscience. That is the way of life. - Didache 4:14

Operation of The Assembly

How is it then, brethren? when ye come together, every one of you hath a psalm, hath a doctrine, hath a tongue, hath a revelation, hath an interpretation. Let all things be done unto edifying. If any man speak in an unknown tongue, let it be by two, or at the most by three, and that by course; and let one interpret. But if there be no interpreter, let him keep silence in the church; and let him speak to himself, and to God.   Let the prophets speak two or three, and

EK-KLĀ-SĒ'-Ä - Operation

let the other judge. If any thing be revealed to another that sitteth by, let the first hold his peace. For ye may all prophesy one by one, that all may learn, and all may be comforted. And the spirits of the prophets are subject to the prophets. For God is not the author of confusion, but of peace, as in all churches of the saints. 1 Corinthians 14:26-33 (KJV)

The New Testament church operates best when agape love is present. Without love we would be better to stay home nothing else matters in the long run. This is a call to return to the operation of a New Testament fellowship where we have equality of leadership, and solid bible teaching that equips the saints to do the work of the ministry. Where the manifestations of the Spirit are true and not fabricated. Where we worship the Lord in Spirit and in truth. Where we have an awareness of our brothers and sisters. Where the widows and orphans are provided for each day. Where outreach is the norm and Christians are know in the community for their love not for their doctrine or their seeker friendly services.

We are entering a very perilous time. We must be prepared to follow the Lord at all costs. Prosperity and me oriented preaching will not suffice for what is about to be unleashed on the true church of God. The times of the gentiles are coming to a close. The true believer will be persecuted as we fail to bend to the ways of the world. As the light of the true church gets dimmer, darkness will increase and if you will live Godly you will suffer persecution because your light will be too bright in the ever increasing darkness.

EK-KLĀ-SĒ'-Ä - Operation

1 - Pictures of the Apostolic Church: Studies in the Book of Acts by William M. Ramsay - Kessinger Publishing
2 - The Way of Agape: Understanding God's Love by Nancy Missler and Chuck Missler - King's High Way
3 - The apostolic preaching and its developments, C. H Dodd - Harper & Row
4 - Dayenu - A Christian view of the Passover - T.M. Cocklin - Worlds of Wonder Publishing
5 - Dr. Arnold Fruchtenbaum - http://www.ariel.org/
6 - Jacob Prasch - http://www.moriel.org/
7 - The Brown-Driver-Briggs Hebrew and English Lexicon - Francis Brown, S. R. Driver, Charles A. Briggs - Hendrickson Publishing
8 - The Amplified Bible - Zondervan Publishing
9 - Expanded Translation - Kenneth Wuest - Eerdmans Publishing.
10 - The Catholic Encyclopedia. New York: Robert Appleton Company
11 - Vines Expositor Dictionary of New Testament Words - by W.E. Vine and Merrill F. Unger
12 - Complete Word Study Bible - by Dr. Warren Patrick Baker D.R.E. and Dr. Spiros Zodhiates
13 - Jacob Prasch - Recording on Divine Healing - a Biblical Understanding

EK-KLĀ-SĒ'-Ä - Operation

THE CHURCH HISTORY OF EUSEBIUS
Chapter V.—The Time of his Appearance among Men.

1. And now, after this necessary introduction to our proposed history of the Church, we can enter, so to speak, upon our journey, beginning with the appearance of our Saviour in the flesh. And we invoke God, the Father of the Word, and him, of whom we have been speaking, Jesus Christ himself our Saviour and Lord, the heavenly Word of God, as our aid and fellow-laborer in the narration of the truth.

2. It was in the forty-second year of the reign of Augustus and the twenty-eighth after the subjugation of Egypt and the death of Antony and Cleopatra, with whom the dynasty of the Ptolemies in Egypt came to an end, that our Saviour and Lord Jesus Christ was born in Bethlehem of Judea, according to the prophecies which had been uttered concerning him. His birth took place during the first census, while Cyrenius was governor of Syria.

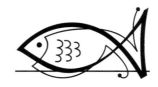

A Brief History of The ekklāsē'ä

Unless otherwise stated all quotes from the early church fathers are taken from books in public domain from the Christian Classics Ethereal Library. Their website link is: www.ccel.org

EK-KLĀ-SĒ'-Ä - A Brief history of The Church

In order to properly understand the bible and its prophecy we must think like a Hebrew. To a Jew prophecy is pattern, it is not strictly prediction and fulfillment. Something may repeat itself but has an ultimate fulfillment. Take for instance

> *And was there until the death of Herod: that it might be fulfilled which was spoken of the Lord by the prophet, saying, Out of Egypt have I called my son. Matthew 2:15*
>
> *When Israel was a child, then I loved him, and called my son out of Egypt. Hosea 11:1*

If you read the context of Hosea 11:1 you would come to the conclusion that Matthew had made a mistake. There is nothing about the Messiah in that chapter. But the pattern of the prophecy played out several times. Abraham was called out of Egypt, Israel was called out, Mary, Joseph and Yeshua were called out and figuratively we are called out of Egypt a type of the world.

How did we get where we are today? We will review seven periods of time based on the seven churches of Revelation. It would appear that the Holy Spirit's intent was to layout in advance the history of the church:

1. Ephesus ~ 33 AD
2. Smyrna ~ 100 AD
3. Pergamos ~ 313 AD
4. Thyatria ~ 600 AD
5. Sardis ~ 1300 AD
6. Philadelphia ~ 1700
7. Laodicea ~ 1800s

I recommend the book by Sir William Ramsay (1851-1939) "*The letters to the Seven Churches of Asia*" you can read this book for free at www.ccel.org. Ramsay does a thorough job of investigation of the seven churches. These were seven literal churches that existed during the time John was writing the Revelation.

We have seen over and over again, what started out correctly soon becomes corrupted by the influence of the world. But, we also see that there was always a remnant of true believers who refused to follow Satan and his evil minions into error. This is a very brief look at our history, the errors and maybe how we can avoid them in the future.

1. Ephesus   "apostolic church" ~ 33AD
Preoccupied with doing, but losing their first love.

> *Unto the angel of the church of Ephesus write; These things saith he that holdeth the seven stars in his right hand, who walketh in the midst of the seven golden candlesticks;* **_I know thy works, and thy labour, and thy patience, and how thou canst not bear them which are evil: and thou hast tried them which say they are apostles, and are not, and hast found them liars: And hast borne, and hast patience, and for my name's sake hast laboured, and hast not fainted._** *Nevertheless I have somewhat against thee, because thou hast left thy first love. Remember therefore from whence thou art fallen, and repent, and do the first works; or else I will come unto thee quickly, and will remove thy candlestick out of his place, except thou repent. But this thou hast, that thou hatest the deeds of the Nicolaitans, which I also hate. He that hath an ear, let him hear what the Spirit saith unto the churches; To him that overcometh will I give to eat of the tree of life, which is in the midst of the paradise of God. Revelation 2:1-7 (KJV)*

During this period we see men of error beginning to sow seeds of doubt and unbelief among the ek-klā-sē'-ä . God tells the Ephesians that He recognizes the fact that they are diligent in the Word and have exposed those who said they are sent by God and are not. Paul knew that there would be perverse men who would come after him and try to destroy the sheep. He tells the elders that they must feed the sheep. I do not think he meant feed them junk food such as pop psychology, prosperity and self-improvement teachings like those found in most churches these days.

We know the Apostles from reading the New Testament. We accept their words as scripture because they knew the Lord personally, except for Paul who had a very significant experience with the Lord and was contemporaries with the other apostles. Then there were the apostolic fathers who knew or were discipled by the apostles. The importance of these early Christian writers is in their confirmation of what the scriptures taught and the historical perspective they give us. There are three apostolic fathers that we know of by their writing who were disciples of the original Apostles they are; Clement of Rome, Ignatius and Polycarp. There are other writers of note from that same period but we are not sure of their relationship to the original apostles. As we unfold the history of the early New Testament, we will reference some of their work. Be aware that what they say is not necessarily always 100% correct. It is important that we compare what they say with the Word, otherwise we run the risk of following a similar path of error.

Solomon said "there is nothing new under the sun". The modern day cults like Jehovah Witnesses and others actually have their roots from early Christian cults of the first centuries, under different names of course. The writers in the first three centuries spoke about different groups who were following the leadership of heretics.

We have learned that Simon Magus, who tried to buy the right to baptize people in the Spirit, is known as the father of Gnosticism. The Gnostics believed that they had a special knowledge outside of the Word. It is clear that cults all use this technique to deceive the believer. The Mormons have their bible, the Jehovah Witnesses have their Watchtower and now the homosexual faction has their Queen James version. Every Christian cult must have special knowledge outside the Word in order to deceive. To entice the believer it must have a modicum of truth so they mix the truth with error. Only those who are throughly familiar with the truth will see the error. It is not my intent here to go into detail as to what they believe, that would take a much larger volume.

The gnostics did miraculous things and used occult practices to achieve their ends.

> the mystic priests belonging to this sect both lead profligate lives and practice magical arts, each one to the extent of his ability. They use exorcisms and incantations. Love-potions, too, and charms, as well as those beings who are called "Paredri" (familiars) and "Oniropompi" (dream-senders), and whatever other curious arts can be had recourse to,

are eagerly pressed into their service. They also have an image of Simon fashioned after the likeness of Jupiter, and another of Helena in the shape of Minerva; and these they worship. Irenæus *Against Heresies Book 1* Chapter 23 *Doctrines and practices of Simon Magus and Menander*

Was Simon the first to declare that he is the Christ? Now after He was taken up again to the Father, there arose some, saying, "I am Christ," like Simon Magus and the rest, whose names we have not time at present to mention Hippolytus. *On the End of the World,* Chapter 9.

This then was the beginning of Satan's attack on the true ek-klā-sē'-ä . The local leadership must be in the habit of equipping the saints with the whole counsel of God and the building up of the body to avoid error coming into the ek-klā-sē'-ä . This requires a plurality of leadership completely dedicated to overseeing the flock so one man does not have final authority.

I know thy works, and thy labour, and thy patience, and how thou canst not bear them which are evil: and thou hast tried them which say they are apostles, and are not, and hast found them liars:

Even before the apostles breathed their last breath the battle for truth had begun. The gnostics with their leader Satan have attacked the truth of the Word from the start. These cults continue today by mixing truth with error.

2. Smyrna ~100 AD

And unto the angel of the church in Smyrna write; These things saith the first and the last, which was dead, and is alive; I know thy works, and tribulation, and poverty, (but thou art rich) and I know the blasphemy of them which say they are Jews, and are not, but are the synagogue of Satan. **<u>Fear none of those things which thou shalt suffer: behold, the devil shall cast some of you into prison, that ye may be tried; and ye shall have tribulation ten days: be thou faithful unto death, and I will give thee a crown of life</u>**. *He that hath an ear, let him hear what the Spirit saith unto the churches; He that overcometh shall not be hurt of the second death. Revelation 2:8-11 (KJV)*

Foxes Book of Martyrs tells us that there were 10 Roman emperors who blamed the Christians for all the trouble in the world. Christians became the scapegoats. These 10 were Nero 61AD, Domitian 81AD, Trajan 108AD, Marcus Aurelius 162AD, Septimus Severus 192AD, Maximinus 235AD, Decius 249AD, Valerian 257AD, Aurelian 274AD and Diocletian (the worst of all) 303AD. Could this be the 10 days spoken about Smyrna in Revelation? This persecution happened over three centuries until the Edict of Milan issued by Emperors Constantine the Great and Licinius in 313 AD.

Paul was well aware of the fact that heresy was creeping in and warned the overseers to feed the flock the full Word of God.

> *For I have not shunned to declare unto you all the counsel of God. Take heed therefore unto yourselves, and to all the flock, over the which the Holy Ghost hath made you overseers, to feed the church of God, which he hath purchased with his own blood. For **I know this, that after my departing shall grievous wolves enter in among you, not sparing the flock.** Also of your own selves shall men arise, speaking perverse things, to draw away disciples after them. Therefore watch, and remember, that by the space of three years I ceased not to warn every one night and day with tears. Acts 20:27-30 (KJV)*

The Jewish Simon bar Kokhba Revolt 132 AD — bar Kokhba was claimed to be the Messiah. Just as Yeshua predicted there would come after him those who claim to be the Messiah. If the book of Daniel is correct then anyone claiming to be the Messiah would have to have come and been cut off before the destruction of the temple in 70AD. Bar Kokhba did not fit the prophecy.

> As Bar Kokhba was formally declared Messiah, the early believers in Yeshua would not join in with his uprising, as it would imply they supported Bar Kochba's messianic claims. This was where the formal split between Judaism and Christianity began. The Bar Kokhba rebellion saw Jewish believers in Yeshua fully excluded from the Jewish community for the first time. In the end, Bar Kokhba was defeated and his followers lost the war, and many were brutally slain by the Romans. Bar Kochba, which meant 'Son of the Star',

was renamed Bar Kozeba – Son of Disappointment.
From: *Shimon Bar Kokhba & The First Tempation of Yeshua*
http://roshpinaproject.com/2010/02/17/shimon-bar-kokhba-the-first-tempation-of-yeshua/

There were many heresies that sprang up during this period.

Marcionism 129 AD - believed that the God of the Old Testament was Not the God of the New.

> According to Marcion, the god of the Old Testament, whom he called the Demiurge, the creator of the material universe, is a jealous tribal deity of the Jews, whose law represents legalistic reciprocal justice and who punishes mankind for its sins through suffering and death. Contrastingly, the god that Jesus professed is an altogether different being, a universal god of compassion and love who looks upon humanity with benevolence and mercy. Marcion also produced his Antitheses contrasting the Demiurge of the Old Testament with the Heavenly Father of the New Testament
> http://en.wikipedia.org/wiki/Marcion_of_Sinope

Marcion Forbids Marriage.
> The flesh is not, according to Marcion, immersed in the water of the sacrament, unless it be(Free from all matrimonial impurity) in virginity, widowhood, or celibacy, or has purchased by divorce a title to baptism, as if even generative impotents did not all receive their flesh from nuptial union. Now, such a scheme as this must no doubt involve the proscription of marriage. Tertullian - Anti-Marcion Chapter 29.—*Marcion Forbids Marriage. Tertullian Eloquently Defends It as Holy, and Carefully Discriminates Between Marcion's Doctrine and His Own Montanism.*

But Paul makes it clear that we should not deny marriage.

> *Now the Spirit speaketh expressly, that in the latter times some shall depart from the faith, giving heed to seducing spirits, and doctrines of devils; Speaking lies in hypocrisy; having their conscience seared with a hot iron;* **Forbidding to marry***, and commanding to*

> *abstain from meats, which God hath created to be received with thanksgiving of them which believe and know the truth*
> *1 Timothy 4:1-3*

There were other heretics in this time frame, too many to include in this book.

3. Pergamos ~ 313AD

The compromised church under Constantine who combined Christianity and Paganism. We could write volumes about what happened under Constantine and Augustine but for our purposes here we will be brief.

> *And to the angel of the church in Pergamos write; These things saith he which hath the sharp sword with two edges; I know thy works, and where thou dwellest, even where Satan's seat is: and thou holdest fast my name, and hast not denied my faith, even in those days wherein Antipas was my faithful martyr, who was slain among you, where Satan dwelleth. But* **<u>I have a few things against thee, because thou hast there them that hold the doctrine of Balaam, who taught Balac to cast a stumblingblock before the children of Israel, to eat things sacrificed unto idols, and to commit fornication. So hast thou also them that hold the doctrine of the Nicolaitans, which thing I hate.</u>** *Repent; or else I will come unto thee quickly, and will fight against them with the sword of my mouth. He that hath an ear, let him hear what the Spirit saith unto the churches; To him that overcometh will I give to eat of the hidden manna, and will give him a white stone, and in the stone a new name written, which no man knoweth saving he that receiveth it.*
> *Revelation 2:12-17 (KJV)*

> "For at least a thousand years before the Reformation the true church was composed of multitudes of simple Christians who were not part of the Roman system. That such believers existed, refused to be called 'Catholics,' and worshiped independently of the Roman hierarchy is history. It is a fact that they were pursued to imprisonment and death since at least the end of the fourth century." (*A Woman Rides the Beast*, by Dave Hunt, p. 254)

EK-KLĀ-SĒ'-Ä - A Brief history of The Church

Constantine 306 AD - This was the beginning of the end for true Christianity. We still hold to many of the beliefs and traditions of this era which are the mixing of Christianity and the Pagan world. Satan's plan is always to water down the believer and mix him/her with error. Constantine was very crafty and made both pagan and Christian comfortable with the heresy. The Edict of Tolerance made Christianity legal. This in effect made Christianity a religion and the personal relationship the believer had was no longer necessary. This is what my concern has been throughout the book. The church has made it possible to "feel" like they have a relationship with the Lord, but in fact the structure has eliminated the need for a personal relationship and replaced it with liturgy and formal structure. This makes it appear as if there is a relationship, when, in fact, the only relationship is that with the "church". Constantine outlawed home fellowships and replaced them with state run "churches" run by state ordained ministers, Christian or not many of them were definitely not true believers.

Aurelius Augustine 354 AD Augustine finished off the New Testament Church with a multitude of heresies. I have listed just a few:

Baptism - baptism was instituted to wash away "original sin," the guilt we inherited at conception.

Infant Baptism - Infants not baptized are eternally damned.

Predestination and irresistible grace - God predetermines some people to damnation and some for salvation. Calvin got his doctrine from Augustine.

Forgiveness - There is no forgiveness outside of the Roman Catholic church.

Purgatory - There is a purging fire after death.

Millennium - claimed that there was no 1000 year reign

Augustine had many other heresies. Along with Constantine, Augustine contributed to the destruction of the true New Testament Church. Augustine started what would become the dark ages for 1200 years the people were without the Word of God and oppressed by the Catholic church. That is not to say that there wasn't a remnant of true believers, God always has a remnant. However, much like today those who hold to the original and unadulterated Word of God are being overwhelmed by the rapidly emerging apostasy.

The Arians

The doctrines of Arius deny that Jesus was God and believed instead that he was only a created being.

> The author of the Arian heresy was Arius, a native of Lybia, and a priest of Alexandria, who, in A.D. 318, began to publish his errors. He was condemned by a council of Lybian and Egyptian bishops, and that sentence was confirmed by the Council of Nice, A.D. 325. After the death of Constantine the Great, the Arians found means to ingratiate themselves into the favor of the emperor Constantinus, his son and successor in the east; and hence a persecution was raised against the orthodox bishops and clergy. The celebrated Athanasius, and other bishops, were banished, and their sees filled with Arians. *Fox's Book of Martyrs* - John Fox.

There were many cults and heretics that sprang up during this time that grew out of the gnostics. I only mention a few here but like all ages there are a number of false cults that arise. The interesting thing is that there is no new belief only the same Satanic lies warmed over. These were: Menander, Ebionites, Nicolaitanes, Carpocrates, Cerinthus, Valentinus just to name a few.

4. Thyatria ~600 AD

The dark ages when the development of the Roman Catholic church was filled with pagan rituals and practices.

> *And unto the angel of the church in Thyatira write; These things saith the Son of God, who hath his eyes like unto a flame of fire, and his feet are like fine brass; I know thy works, and charity, and service, and faith, and thy patience, and thy works; and the last to be more than the first. Notwithstanding I have a few things against thee,* **because thou sufferest that woman Jezebel, which calleth herself a prophetess, to teach and to seduce my servants to commit fornication, and to eat things sacrificed unto idols. And I gave her space to repent of her fornication; and she repented not. Behold, I will cast her into a bed, and them that commit adultery with her into great tribulation, except they repent of**

their deeds. And I will kill her children with death; and all the churches shall know that I am he which searcheth the reins and hearts: and I will give unto every one of you according to your works. *But unto you I say, and unto the rest in Thyatira, as many as have not this doctrine, and which have not known the depths of Satan, as they speak; I will put upon you none other burden. But that which ye have already hold fast till I come. And he that overcometh, and keepeth my works unto the end, to him will I give power over the nations: And he shall rule them with a rod of iron; as the vessels of a potter shall they be broken to shivers: even as I received of my Father. And I will give him the morning star. He that hath an ear, let him hear what the Spirit saith unto the churches. Revelation 2:18-29 (KJV)*

Waldenses - opposing Papal Authority

In A.D. 1147, because of Henry of Toulouse, deemed their most eminent preacher, they were called Henericians; and as they would not admit of any proofs relative to religion, but what could be deduced from the Scriptures themselves, the popish party gave them the name of apostolics. At length, Peter Waldo, or Valdo, a native of Lyons, eminent for his piety and learning, became a strenuous opposer of popery; and from him the reformed, at that time, received the appellation of Waldenses or Waldoys.

Pope Alexander III being informed by the bishop of Lyons of these transactions, excommunicated Waldo and his adherents, and commanded the bishop to exterminate them, if possible, from the face of the earth; hence began the papal persecutions against the Waldenses.

The proceedings of Waldo and the reformed, occasioned the first rise of the inquisitors; for Pope Innocent III authorized certain monks as inquisitors, to inquire for, and deliver over, the reformed to the secular power. The process was short, as an accusation was deemed adequate to guilt, and a candid trial was never granted to the accused.

The pope, finding that these cruel means had not the intended effect, sent several learned monks to preach among the Waldenses, and to endeavor to argue them out of their opinions. Among these monks was one Dominic, who appeared extremely zealous in the cause of popery. This Dominic instituted an order, which, from him, was called the order of Dominican friars; and the members of this order have ever since been the principal inquisitors in the various inquisitions in the world. The power of the inquisitors was unlimited; they proceeded against whom they pleased, without any consideration of age, sex, or rank.
Fox's Book Of Martyrs - John Fox

Albigenses - Correcting error

The reformation of papistical error very early was projected in France; for in the third century a learned man, named Almericus, and six of his disciples, were ordered to be burnt at Paris for asserting that God was no otherwise present in the sacramental bread than in any other bread; that it was idolatry to build altars or shrines to saints and that it was ridiculous to offer incense to them.

A native of Malda was burnt by a slow fire, for saying that Mass was a plain denial of the death and passion of Christ.
Fox's Book Of Martyrs - John Fox

The Beginning of the Inquisition

The most zealous of all the popish monks, and those who most implicitly obeyed the Church of Rome, were the Dominicans and Franciscans: these, therefore, the pope thought proper to invest with an exclusive right of presiding over the different courts of Inquisition, and gave them the most unlimited powers, as judges delegated by him, and immediately representing his person: they were permitted to excommunicate, or sentence to death whom they thought proper, upon the most slight information of heresy. They were allowed to publish crusades against all

whom they deemed heretics, and enter into leagues with sovereign princes, to join their crusades with their forces. In 1244, their power was further increased by the emperor Frederic II, who declared himself the protector and friend of all the inquisitors, and published the cruel edicts, viz., 1. That all heretics who continue obstinate, should be burnt. 2. That all heretics who repented, should be imprisoned for life.
Fox's Book Of Martyrs - John Fox

5. Sardis ~ 1300 AD

The reformation when the doctrines of the Roman Catholic church were questioned. However, the protestant church was not all that it could have been, it held to a lot of the heresy of the Roman Catholic church. It eventually became dead as we see today.

> *And unto the angel of the church in Sardis write; These things saith he that hath the seven Spirits of God, and the seven stars;* <u>**I know thy works, that thou hast a name that thou livest, and art dead.**</u> *Be watchful, and strengthen the things which remain, that are ready to die: for I have not found thy works perfect before God. Remember therefore how thou hast received and heard, and hold fast, and repent. If therefore thou shalt not watch, I will come on thee as a thief, and thou shalt not know what hour I will come upon thee.* <u>**Thou hast a few names even in Sardis which have not defiled their garments; and they shall walk with me in white: for they are worthy.**</u> *He that overcometh, the same shall be clothed in white raiment; and I will not blot out his name out of the book of life, but I will confess his name before my Father, and before his angels. He that hath an ear, let him hear what the Spirit saith unto the churches. Revelation 3:1-6 (KJV)*

The Reformation

If it were not for Fredrick III Elector of Saxony 1 the reformation may not have ever been possible. Known as Frederick the Wise, Fredrick III protected Martin Luther from being executed by the Catholics even though he was a Catholic until his death. Without his help and the strength of his army Luther would never have survived to correct some of the heresy propagated by the catholic church like justification by faith. That is not to say that Luther did all he could because he held to many of the doctrines of Augustine like infant baptism and other heresies. He was also vehemently anti-Semitic as seen in the following quotes.

> In 1543 Luther published On the Jews and Their Lies in which he says that the Jews are a "base, whoring people, that is, no people of God, and their boast of lineage, circumcision, and law must be accounted as filth."[1] They are full of the "devil's feces ... which they wallow in like swine."[2]

After Luther had been placed under the imperial ban by the diet at Worms, the elector caused him to be conveyed to his castle at the Wartburg, and afterwards protected him while he attacked the enemies of the Reformation. *http://www.theodora.com/encyclopedia/f/frederick_iii_of_saxony.html*

However, it was the chink in the armor that opened the door for other groups that were not considered Protestant like the Anabaptists. Both Catholics and Protestants alike hated the Anabaptists and others like them.

Without the reformation we may never have escaped the iron fisted rule of the Catholics and may never have been able to read the Word of God for ourselves and seen the truth of the word.

When we think of the Reformation we automatically think of **Martin Luther** as the hero of the time. In reality they did very little in moving from the reign of terror of the Catholic Church. He did correct some errors but left many in place and was adamantly antisemitic. We can attribute the "sola fide" or by faith alone to Luther but little else. When all is said and done Luther still held to many of the Constantine and Augustine errors.

Ulrich Zwingli

Declared that the Bible, not the Pope or the Roman Catholic Church, was the sole authority of the Church. But both Zwingli and Luther were violently opposed to the Ana-baptists over the issue of Infant baptism. They were quite willing to persecute and kill those with whom they disagreed.

EK-KLĀ-SĒ'-Ä - A Brief history of The Church

The Persucuted

The Anabaptists - "one who baptizes over again." The Anabaptists were not Protestants like Luther and Calvin, in fact, it is said, that they opposed them as "fanatics,"—just as bad as the papists. Anabaptists were heavily persecuted by both Protestants and Roman Catholics. They did not have a single leader like Luther who lead them all. They believed that only baptism of an adult who understood repentance was valid and infant baptism did not save you. The Lord's Supper was a memorial and not the crucifixion as in the Catholic Mass. They believed the Bible as the sole rule of faith and practice – the authority of the Scriptures and the Priesthood of all believers. You can see why the Protestants and Catholics had issues with the Anabaptists.

The Anabaptists insisted upon the "free course" of the Holy Spirit in worship, yet still maintained it all must be judged according to the Scriptures.* The Swiss Anabaptist document titled "Answer of Some Who Are Called (Ana-)Baptists – Why They Do Not Attend the Churches". One reason given for not attending the state churches was that these institutions forbade the congregation to exercise spiritual gifts according to "the Christian order as taught in the gospel or the Word of God in 1 Corinthians 14." "When such believers come together, 'Everyone of you (note every one) hath a psalm, hath a doctrine, hath a revelation, hath an interpretation', and so on. When someone comes to church and constantly hears only one person speaking, and all the listeners are silent, neither speaking nor prophesying, who can or will regard or confess the same to be a spiritual congregation, or confess according to 1 Corinthians 14 that God is dwelling and operating in them through His Holy Spirit with His gifts, impelling them one after another in the above-mentioned order of speaking and prophesying.**

*Oyer, John S, Lutheran Reformers Against Anabaptists, The Hague: M Nijhoff, p. 86.

** Peachey, Paul; Peachey, Shem, eds. (1971), "Answer of Some Who Are Called (Ana-)Baptists – Why They Do Not Attend the Churches", Mennonite Quarterly Review 45

The Good

John Wycliffe - Wycliffe is credited with translating the Latin Bible in to middle-English in about 1384. He believed that only the Word of God was the authority not man. He was completely against the belief in transubstantiation (where the wine becomes the blood of Yeshua and the bread actually becomes flesh) as taught by the Catholic Church. Many of his followers were tried and convicted by the church on that basis alone.

Wycliffe trained his followers (*known as Lollards) to go out and preach to the people. Many of these people were burned at the stake and if the scriptures translated by Wycliffe were found on them, they were tied around their necks before burning.

* derogatory nickname given to those without an academic background, educated if at all only in English

Jan Huss - A follower of Wycliffe denied the infallibility of the Pope and declared that the Word was the final authority. He was burned at the stake at the age of 45 as a heretic by the Catholic Church.

> Perhaps he thought, Will I have a legacy? Has my life been in vain? But God had promised: "They will silence the goose (Hus means goose in Czech), but in 100 years I will raise a swan from your ashes that no one will be able to silence."
> "God, give me strength," he prayed. "My hope is in You. I have no strength of my own."
> *Jan Hus:* The Goose of Bohemia* By William P. Farley

100 years later Martin Luther nailed the 95 Thesis to the Wittenburg door. This began the Protestant reformation. Although these men of the reformation questioned the doctrine and practices of the Catholic Church, they were still far from the complete truth. Martin Luther was extreme in his antisemitism among other heresies.

The pace was quickened in 1440 when Gutenberg invented his movable type printing press. Where it would take scribes several months to transcribe one bible, these bibles could be printed in much less time. William Tyndale, Martin Luther and others would have a much greater influence than was possible before the Gutenberg press.

Erasmus was the first in 1515 to create a parallel bible with the Greek text on the left and the Latin translation on the right. This also helped reform thinking at the time because it proved that the Latin Vulgate was faulty. Tyndale in 1526 uses Erasmus' translation to create his English translation.

John Bunyan writes The Pilgrim's Progress 1678 - Bunyan was jailed for violating Conventicle Act which prohibited holding religious services outside of the Church of England and preaching without a license. It is said that Pilgrim's Progress has never been out of print.

The Bad

The formation of the Jesuits with **Ignatius Loyola** as its founder in 1534 was tasked with putting down the reformers and bringing them back under the authority of the church.

> Between 1555 and 1931 the Society of Jesus was expelled from at least 83 countries, city states and cities, for engaging in political intrigue and subversion plots against the welfare of the State, according to the records of a Jesuit priest of repute… Practically every instance of expulsion was for political intrigue, political infiltration, political subversion, and inciting to political insurrection. - J. E. C. Shepherd (Canadian historian), *The Babington Plot: Jesuit Intrigue in Elizabethan England (Toronto, Canada: Wittenburg Publications)*:

The Inquisitions - This was a time of severe persecution of Jews, Protestants and Christians. First by the Dominicans and then The infamous Spanish inquisition of King Ferdinand of Aragon and Queen Isabella of Castile. Then in the sixteenth century the Roman inquisition started and brought many to the fire.

> In the year 1231 Pope Gregory IX appointed the first "inquisitors of heretical depravity" to serve as explicit papal agents. Thus began what is called the Medieval Inquisition, which was launched to deal with the menace posed to the Church by Christian heretics, notably the Cathars of southern France . The newly established Dominican Order, whose priests and nuns are identifiable to this day by their white habits, was instrumental in combating the Cathar heresy. Its founder , Dominic Guzmán, is the man celebrated in the 1963 song "Dominique," by the Singing Nun (said to be the only Belgian song ever to hit No. 1 on the American charts). The inquisitors solicited denunciations and, as their name implies, conducted interrogations . Their efforts were highly localized— there was no central command. The inquisitors were aided in their work by the Papal Bull Ad Extirpanda, promulgated in 1252, which justified and encouraged the use of torture, wielding philosophical arguments that have never

wanted for advocates and that would eventually echo in the White House and the Justice Department. Within a century, the work of the Medieval Inquisition was largely done.
Cullen Murphy - *God's Jury: The Inquisition and the Making of the Modern World* Houghton Mifflin Harcourt.

Two confusing doctrines perpetrated at the time.

Sometimes people will try to correct errors in doctrine by over emphasis of another doctrine. This is what Calvin did in trying to correct what the Catholics were teaching. Below is a comparison of John Calvin (Calvinism) and Jacob Arminius (Arminianism). I do not completely agree with either. Today many Calvinists have softened their beliefs.

Calvin was very much like Luther and Zwingli in following the Augustine doctrine especially concerning predestination. It is clear that Catholics and Protestants alike were still along way from the original New Testament Church structure. The only difference, as it turns out was who was in charge.

Calvinism	Arminianism
Total Depravity - because of the fall no one can not choose for themselves	**Free will** - you are free to choose to believe or not.
Unconditional Election - God has already chosen who will be saved so faith and repentance have no effect.	**Conditional Election** - God foreknew who would accept him. Election therefore was not determined by man.
Limited Atonement - Christ's work on the cross only applies to the elect.	**Universal Redemption** - Only those who believe will be saved.
Irresistible Grace - The call of the Spirit irresistibly draws sinners (Elect) to Christ	**Call of the Holy Spirit** can be Resisted - A person can reject the call to repentance.
Perseverance of the Saints - All who are chosen by God, redeemed by Christ, and given faith by the Spirit are eternally saved.	**Falling from Grace** - Those who believe and are truly saved can lose their salvation by failing to keep up their faith.

6. Philadelphia ~ 1700 AD to ?

Philadelphia is known as the missionary church. It has nothing bad said about it. But where are the great missionary movements of today?

> *And to the angel of the church in Philadelphia write; These things saith he that is holy, he that is true, he that hath the key of David, he that openeth, and no man shutteth; and shutteth, and no man openeth; I know thy works: behold, I have set before thee an open door, and no man can shut it: for thou hast a little strength, and hast kept my word, and hast not denied my name. Behold, I will make them of the synagogue of Satan, which say they are Jews, and are not, but do lie; behold, I will make them to come and worship before thy feet, and to know that I have loved thee. Because thou hast kept the word of my patience, I also will keep thee from the hour of temptation, which shall come upon all the world, to try them that dwell upon the earth. Behold, I come quickly: hold that fast which thou hast, that no man take thy crown. Him that overcometh will I make a pillar in the temple of my God, and he shall go no more out: and I will write upon him the name of my God, and the name of the city of my God, which is new Jerusalem, which cometh down out of heaven from my God: and I will write upon him my new name. He that hath an ear, let him hear what the Spirit saith unto the churches. Revelation 3:7-13 (KJV)*

The First Great Awakening in the United States began in the 1730s Some of the great leaders during this time are:

Jonathan Edwards pastor at Northampton 1729
John & Charles Wesley's evangelical conversions 1738
George Whitefield converted 1735 and was mentored by the Wesleys. He was considered a great orator and drew very large crowds.
J. N. Darby founds the Plymouth Brethren 1827
George Mueller opens Scriptural Knowledge Institute 1834
Charles Spurgeon becomes pastor of New Park St. Church 1854
D. L. Moody converted 1855

Satan unleashes a most powerful deception
Darwin publishes *Origin of Species* 1859. This was not a new thought these

ideas were alive in the first century.

The World is uncreated

>Some of the philosophers of the Porch say that there is no God at all; or, if there is, they say that He cares for none but Himself; and these views the folly of Epicurus and Chrysippus has set forth at large. And others say that all things are produced without external agency, and that the world is uncreated, and that nature is eternal; - Theophilus To Autolycus - Book II. Chapter 4.—*Absurd Opinions Of The Philosophers Concerning God.*

>And saying this, he has not yet explained by whom all this was made. For if chaos existed in the beginning, and matter of some sort, being uncreated, was previously existing, who was it that effected the change on its condition, and gave it a different order and shape? Did matter itself alter its own form and arrange itself into a world (for Jupiter was born, not only long after matter, but long after the world and many men; and so, too, was his father Saturn), or was there some ruling power which made it; I mean, of course, God, who also fashioned it into a world? Theophilus To Autolycus. Book II. Chapter 6.—*Hesiod On The Origin Of The World.*

Men and Animals were not created

>But I cannot here omit that which some erring philosophers say, t**hat men and the other animals arose from the earth without any author**; whence that expression of Virgil:—"And the earth-born race of men raised its head from the hard fields." Lactantius - Divine Institutes - Chap. 11.—*Of living creatures, of man; Prometheus, Deucalion, the Parcæ*

Cavemen

>They have introduced not one origin only, and cause of building a city; but some relate that those men who were first born from the earth, when they passed a wandering life among the woods and plains, and were not united by any

mutual bond of speech or justice, but had leaves and grass for their beds, and caves and grottos for their dwellings, were a prey to the beasts and stronger animals. Lactantius - *Divine Institutes* Chapter 10.—*Of religion towards God, and mercy towards men; and of the beginning*

These quotes are only a few that we could use. The fact is that Satan has been trying to convince man that God did not create the world for a long time. Darwin came at such a time in history that was ripe to accept the lie.

> "Biochemical systems are exceedingly complex, so much so that the chance of their being formed through random shufflings of simple organic molecules is exceedingly minute, to a point where it is insensibly different from zero."
>
> Fred Hoyle and Chandra Wickramasinghe, Evolution from Space (1981), p. 3.

"Darwin's theory, I believe, is on the verge of collapse. In his famous book, Origin of Species, Darwin made a mistake sufficiently serious to undermine his theory. And that mistake has only recently been recognized as such. I have not been surprised to read ... that in some of the latest evolutionary theories 'natural selection plays no role at all.' Darwin, I suggest, is in the process of being discarded ... But perhaps in deference to the venerable old gentleman ... it is being done as discreetly and gently as possible, with a minimum of publicity" Tom Bethell, "Darwin's Mistake," *The Craft of Prose, pp. 311, 314*

Evolutionists want freedom from accountability to God this is the reason they fight so hard to keep evolution alive otherwise they lose the ability to do what ever they want. Listen to Aldos Huxley grandson of Darwin's bulldog Thomas Huxley.

> "I had motives for not wanting the world to have meaning; consequently assumed it had none, and was able without any difficulty to find satisfying reasons for this assumption . .The philosopher who finds no meaning in the world is not

concerned exclusively with a problem In pure metaphysics; he is also concerned to prove there is no valid reason why he personally should not do as he wants to do . . For myself, as no doubt foremost of my contemporaries, the philosophy of meaninglessness was essentially an instrument of liberation. The liberation we desired was simultaneously liberation from a certain political and economic system and liberation from a certain system of morality objected to the morality because it interfered with our sexual freedom." Aldous Huxley."Confessions of a Professed Atheist," Report: Perspective on the News, Vol. 3, June 1966, p. 19

7. Laodicea ~ 1800 AD to the Return?
The liberal apostate church.

> *And unto the angel of the church of the Laodiceans write; These things saith the Amen, the faithful and true witness, the beginning of the creation of God; **I know thy works, that thou art neither cold nor hot: I would thou wert cold or hot. So then because thou art lukewarm, and neither cold nor hot, I will spue thee out of my mouth. Because thou sayest, I am rich, and increased with goods, and have need of nothing; and knowest not that thou art wretched, and miserable, and poor, and blind, and naked: I counsel thee to buy of me gold tried in the fire, that thou mayest be rich; and white raiment, that thou mayest be clothed, and that the shame of thy nakedness do not appear; and anoint thine eyes with eyesalve, that thou mayest see.** As many as I love, I rebuke and chasten: be zealous therefore, and repent. Behold, I stand at the door, and knock: if any man hear my voice, and open the door, I will come in to him, and will sup with him, and he with me. To him that overcometh will I grant to sit with me in my throne, even as I also overcame, and am set down with my Father in his throne. He that hath an ear, let him hear what the Spirit saith unto the churches. Revelation 3:14-22 (KJV)*

Christianity in modern America is, in large part, innocuous. It tends to be easy, upbeat, convenient , and compatible. It does not require self sacrifice, discipline, humility, an otherworldly outlook, a zeal for souls, a fear as well as

> love of God. There is little guilt and no punishment, and
> the payoff in heaven is virtually certain. The faith has
> been overwhelmed by the culture, producing what may be
> called cultural Christianity . . . [that is] when the faith is
> dominated by a culture to the point that it loses much or
> most of its authenticity . . . What we now have might be best
> labeled Consumer Christianity . . . Millions of Americans
> today feel free to buy as much of the full Christian faith as
> seems desirable. The cost is low and customer satisfaction
> seems guaranteed . . . America is not – not yet, anyway – a
> thoroughly secular society. But its Christianity, in large part,
> has been watered down and is at ease with basic secular
> premises about personal conduct and the meaning of life.
> Such a religion has an uncertain future for it has absorbed
> ideas and attitudes that may well lead to its demise . Authentic
> Christianity and the world are by definition at odds, - by
> Thomas C. Reeves - *The Empty Church: Does Organized
> Religion Matter Anymore?*, The Free Press, 1996, pp. 66,67.

The nineteenth century saw the resurgence of the Humanist movement in a big way due to the lie which is now known as Darwinism and a growing antisemitism brought on by the church itself because of replacement theology. Replacement theology states that Israel has been replaced by the church. This is a complete fabrication and lie. Paul addresses this head on in Romans 11. Charismatics are famous for taking this verse out of context and applying it to themselves. He is talking about the Jewish people and their relationship to God **_NOT_** gifts that the Holy Spirit may have given them.

> *For I would not, brethren, that ye should be ignorant of this
> mystery, lest ye should be wise in your own conceits; that blindness
> in part is happened to Israel, until the fullness of the Gentiles be
> come in. And so all Israel shall be saved: as it is written, There shall
> come out of Sion the Deliverer, and shall turn away ungodliness
> from Jacob: For this is my covenant unto them, when I shall take
> away their sins. As concerning the gospel, they are enemies for your
> sakes: but as touching the election, they are beloved for the fathers'
> sakes.* **_For the gifts and calling of God are without repentance_**.
> *Romans 11:25-29 (KJV)*

The 20th and 21st centuries had been the bloodiest in all of History. Beginning with the first World War I. Then came World War II under Hitler in Germany and Hirohito as Emperor of Japan. Hitler slaughtered six million Jews. Add to that number those who were executed under Stalin. Soviet archives and historians now estimate that nearly 700,000 people were executed in the course of his reign. And don't forget Benito Mussolini who killed 300,000 of his own people. This was just the beginning of sorrows. In the 1950s, we had the Korean War and in the 1960s and 1970s the Vietnam War. Not to mention the wars against Israel in 1948, 1967, 1974 and so on continuing to this day. We have wars and rumor of wars all around us.

Now the birth pangs and intensity are increasing as we see the resurgence of the Muslim faith across the world. Daily we are hearing of Christians and Jews being slaughtered in the name of the moon god, Allah. But also Muslims of differing Muslim factions are murdering other Muslims. It would be as if Conservative Baptists were killing Southern Baptists. There are so many things we could discuss but it is only my intent to give a very brief review of what has and is happening from the 19th century until today.

William Booth - (deceased August 20, 1912) The Salvation Army in the early years was very evangelical in their outreach. He taught that hell was real and repentance from sin was necessary for salvation. This group was hated and mocked in the public square. His mission was to the poor. He was criticized for using secular tunes to attract a crowd. (Not unlike the Jesus music of the 60s and 70s). He once said,

> "While women weep, as they do now, I'll fight; while little children go hungry, I'll fight; while men go to prison, in and out, in and out, as they do now, I'll fight—while there is a drunkard left, while there is a poor lost girl upon the streets, where there remains one dark soul without the light of God—I'll fight! I'll fight to the very end!"

In the early 20th century there was an outpouring of the Holy Spirit which birthed the Pentecostal movement.

EK-KLĀ-SĒ'-Ä - A Brief history of The Church

Charles Parham was born in Muscatine, Iowa (I only mention it because I was born there as well.) on June 4, 1873. Parham had many physical maladies among them rheumatic fever. At the age of 15 he started having evangelistic meetings. He had an intense desire to learn about divine healing and followed Wesleyan holiness. Parham had visited many of the great men of his era; Dowie's Healing homes in Chicago, D. L. Moody, A.B. Simpson among others. He started a school in Kansas in 1900 but it closed when the building was taken over by someone else. Eventually he open a bible school in Houston. Attending the school was William Seymour who would lead the Azusa Street Revival.

In the mid 20th century another movement of the Holy Spirit resulted in the Charismatics. This by no means is an exhaustive list but these are ones of special note.

Chuck Smith (deceased October 3, 2013) and the Calvary Chapels. Chuck was a man of vision and invited the counter-culture youth into his church. Many Christian rock groups came out of Calvary Chapel and was a hub of the Jesus people movement. I was privileged to have gone to Calvary Chapel when they were still meeting in a tent. Calvary Chapel made it a habit of teaching the word verse by verse.

Derek Prince (deceased 24 September 2003) Derek was one of my first mentors via cassette tape. I only saw him once in Miami, Florida, but he has had a profound effect on me and many others who have sat under his teaching. You can still benefit from his teaching ministry in books and on the Internet. Bob Mumford also had a huge impact on my early Christian life through tapes as well.

David Wilkerson (deceased April 27, 2011) - David was famous for going into the worst neighborhoods in New York City to preach the gospel. One of his converts was Nicky Cruz from which came the movie Cross and the Switchblade. David was a prophet and a true man of God and founder of the addiction recovery program Teen Challenge.

Jewish roots - This is a very necessary and missing piece in most churches today. Our faith comes from the foundation of the Jewish faith. Jesus was a Jew, the early Christians were all Jews. As gentiles we have been grafted into the vine. We must not neglect our Jewish roots, however, that is not to say that all Messianic fellowships are completely correct in their doctrine. There are some Messianic fellowships which are right on. I personally look to Jacob Prasch and Dr. Arnold Fruchtenbaum when I need clarification on Messianic issues. Jews for Jesus is also a good organization. There are many Messianic fellowships being started, just be aware of their foundational doctrine and do not get caught up in strictly keeping the law.

TV Evangelism: a good idea gone bad.
Like many movements throughout history the beginning is good but over time error creeps in and eventually destroys the very thing that it started out to do bringing shame on Christians and the Lord who bought us. I am going to make generalized statements now that does not mean that everyone is the same, there are good mixed with very bad.

Christian TV is big business and most of these TV networks and shows make their founders and speakers very wealthy from offerings, and the sale of books and media. I just can not see the biblical basis for getting rich selling the gospel and then yearly begging for money to keep it going; all in the name of "sowing into God's work". The early church did not have the communication capabilities we have today and yet the church grew astronomically. Once again, the responsibility and obligation of each Christian for personal witness and evangelism is given over to the TV evangelist who cannot disciple anyone. Does all of this TV really result in lives being changed and believers being discipled? Does their teaching result in the building up of the body? For the amount of money that is poured into these organizations what is the return on investment? It is far better to have "boots on the ground" to use a military term, like the missionaries who have direct contact with people and not through the one way communication of the "one eyed monster".

The issue is that you get false teachers and prophets mixed in with true. If I put a red poison in a glass of water and tell you that only the red part is poison so be careful not to swallow the poison when you drink it, you would tell me that I am crazy because you cannot separate the good from the bad when it is mixed. Aha! You are right! Can you tell when a person is a false teacher or prophet? Not always, because they mix enough truth with the error to make it palatable. This is the reason that the ek-klā-sē'-ä must teach the Word and equip the saints to do the work of the ministry. The leaders in the church are to watch over the flock to keep the wolves from

EK-KLĀ-SĒ'-Ä - A Brief history of The Church

feeding on it. I wish there was no Christian TV. It makes watching over the flock so much more difficult. Teaching belongs in the local fellowship where men are held accountable for what is taught by other men who are also accountable for oversight and feeding the flock.

There is a group emerging that tells its people not to study end time prophecy because they won't understand it anyway. Better to concentrate on world peace and feeding the poor. Doing good works is not a bad thing, we are told to do it. But neglecting the Word and discipleship will lead to a weak and vulnerable sheep. The Lord tells us to watch for the end and pray.

> *But of that day and that hour knoweth no man, no, not the angels which are in heaven, neither the Son, but the Father. Take ye heed, watch and pray: for ye know not when the time is. Mark 13:32-33*

> *And take heed to yourselves, lest at any time your hearts be overcharged with surfeiting, and drunkenness, and cares of this life, and so that day come upon you unawares. For as a snare shall it come on all them that dwell on the face of the whole earth. Watch ye therefore, and pray always, that ye may be accounted worthy to escape all these things that shall come to pass, and to stand before the Son of man. Luke 21:34-36*

There is a growing trend to seek out the supernatural. I believe in the supernatural power of God and miracles still happen today, healing, raising the dead among others. However, an over emphasis on the supernatural can lead to serious error. We know from 2 Timothy 3:8 that Jannes and Jambres were able to replicate the miracles that Moses preformed before Pharaoh. We have learned that in the early church Simon Magus also did miracles and deceived many. In Revelation, we are told that the false prophet will do false signs and wonders in the last days. We must be very careful of chasing signs and wonders, it is a trap that Satan can use to snare unsuspecting believers. Just because it is supernatural does not mean its origination is from God. It says that signs and wonders "follow" not our following after them. Chasing them will eventually lead to serious error.

> *And **these signs shall follow** them that believe; In my name shall they cast out devils; they shall speak with new tongues; They shall*

take up serpents; and if they drink any deadly thing, it shall not hurt them; they shall lay hands on the sick, and they shall recover. Mark 16:17-18 (KJV)

I think that we are at the beginning of a new reformation where true believers will turn away from the apostate church. Not just the Catholic Church but against the heresy of the modern Protestant churches and others like non-denominational churches that have strayed and abandoned the truth of the pure Word of God. This will result in persecution for the remnant from the apostate organizations. As the light of truth is shown on their lies and deceptions, they will react violently. As true believers in the truth of the Word of God, we will be lied about and falsely accused. As their darkness increases so will their hate for the remnant. The true believers will go underground just like the first century Christians. I believe that history will repeat itself.

May God bless you and keep you in the coming days!

EK-KLĀ-SĒ'-Ä - A Brief history of The Church

1- Luther, Martin. On the Jews and Their Lies, 154, 167, 229, cited in Michael, Robert. Holy Hatred: Christianity, Antisemitism, and the Holocaust. New York: Palgrave Macmillan, 2006, p. 111.

2- Obermann, Heiko. Luthers Werke. Erlangen 1854, 32:282, 298, in Grisar, Hartmann. Luther. St. Louis 1915, 4:286 and 5:406, cited in Michael, Robert. Holy Hatred: Christianity, Antisemitism, and the Holocaust. New York: Palgrave Macmillan, 2006, p. 113.

Recommended resources for personal study.

Teachers

Although I do not always agree with everything these men say, except in their foundational doctrine. They are the "best in class" for today. This is my short list of solid Bible teachers it is in no way exhaustive only ones I have found to be solid in their beliefs. Regardless, we should always confirm everything someone says with the scripture. It is especially true today since we are in the age of apostasy. There are, however, aspects of the scripture which are not absolutely clear; when the rapture will occur for instance. In these cases we must research but as the apostolic fathers said we should not be divided over these issues but continue to search the scriptures.

(In alphabetic order)
Teachers generally good solid Bible teachers with a long history of foundational truth.

David Hocking
davidhocking.org
Hope for Today was founded by Dr. David Hocking in the fall of 1995. David was born in Long Beach, CA and after High School, attended Bob Jones University in Greenville, SC, where he graduated with a B.A. in Bible, Greek, and Ancient History. After college, David attended Grace Theological Seminary in Winona Lake, IN, where he received his M. Div. degree in Biblical Studies. David also continued graduate studies and received a Doctor of Ministry degree as well as a Ph.D. degree in Biblical Studies and languages. David also received a Doctor of Laws degree, being honored by Biola University.

David has been preaching and teaching the Bible for over 50 years and has taught courses in Bible, Theology, Biblical Languages and Expository Preaching in colleges as well as in graduate schools. His radio Bible teaching began in 1970 and has included such programs as Sounds of Grace, The Biola Hour, Solid Rock, and for the last 13 years - Hope for Today. David has served as pastor in Columbus, Ohio, Long Beach, California, and Santa Ana, California. He has written over 35 books

Dave Hunt (deceased April 5, 2013)
thebereancall.org
Dave's book *The Woman Rides the Beast* is an excellent study on the history

and beliefs of the Catholic church. He has many other books and videos on the subject of apologetics. He was most interested in correcting the errors he found in churches and cults.

Walter Martin (deceased June 26, 1989) The Kingdom of the Cults (1965), he has been dubbed the "godfather of the anti-cult movement" by Michael J. McManus, "Eulogy for the godfather of the anti-cult movement", The Free Lance-Star, Fredricksburg, VA,

Chuck Missler
khouse.org
K-House was founded by Chuck and Nancy Missler. Chuck, a Naval academy graduate and former Branch Chief of the Dept. of Guided Missiles, had a remarkable 30-year executive career. He served on the Board of Directors of 12 public companies and was CEO of 6 of them. For twenty years Chuck balanced his high-profile corporate career with his teaching commitment to a weekly Bible study at Calvary Chapel Costa Mesa in Southern California. Nancy, while raising their four children, has touched the lives of thousands through her in-depth teaching of Biblical discoveries in her "Way of Agape" and "Be Ye Transformed" books and tape series.

Watchman Nee (deceased May 30, 1972)
Nee believed in the verbal inspiration of the Bible and that the Bible is God's Word. He also believed that God is triune, Father, Son, and Spirit, distinctly three, yet fully one, co-existing and co-inhering each other from eternity to eternity. He believed that Jesus Christ is the Son of God, even God Himself, incarnated as a man with both the human life and the divine life, that He died on the cross to accomplish redemption, that he rose bodily from the dead on the third day, that He ascended into heaven and was enthroned, crowned with glory, and made the Lord of all, and that He will return the second time to receive His followers, to save Israel, and to establish His millennial kingdom on the earth. He believed that every person who believes in Jesus Christ will be forgiven by God, washed by His redeeming blood, justified by faith, regenerated by the Holy Spirit, and saved by grace. Such a believer is a child of God and a member of the Body of Christ. He also believed that the destiny of every

believer is to be an integral part of the church, which is the Body of Christ and the house of God - *A Seer of the Divine Revelation in the Present Age*. Anaheim: Living Stream Ministry (1991).

Derek Prince (deceased 24 September 2003)
Derek is with the Lord now but his teaching is still available all over the Internet and you-tube. At the time of Prince's death in September 2003, he was the author of over 50 books, 600 audio and 100 video teachings, many of which have been translated and published in more than 100 languages. Some of the subjects that are covered in his teachings are prayer and fasting, foundations of the Christian faith, spiritual warfare, God's love and marriage and family.
As a Pentecostal, Prince believed in the reality of spiritual forces operating in the world, and of the power of demons to cause illness and psychological problems. While in Seattle he was asked to perform an exorcism on a woman, and he came to believe that demons could attack Christians. This was at odds with the more usual Pentecostal view that demons could only affect non-Christians. Prince believed that his deliverance ministry used the power of God to defeat demons. (from http://en.wikipedia.org/wiki/Derek_Prince)

Balanced and solid understand the Jewish background of the New Testament without making people keep the Law. Overall excellent teachers who have a solid grasp of the entire word. There is a movement of Jewish-roots teachers which over-emphasize keeping the Old Testament Law, of these beware. It is very important that we understand that the Bible is a Jewish book, Jesus was a Jew and to properly understand the entire word we must understand the roots of our faith.

Dr. Arnold Fruchtenbaum
http://ariel.org
Upon graduating from high school, Arnold was forced by his father to leave home because of his faith. In 1962, he began undergraduate education at Shelton College in New Jersey. Transferring to Ohio's Cedarville College, he graduated with a Bachelor of Arts degree in Hebrew and Greek in 1966. He then moved to Israel, where he studied archaeology, ancient history, historical geography, and Hebrew at the American Institute of Holy Land Studies and the Hebrew University in Jerusalem. During this time, he witnessed the historic Six-Day War in 1967. Later that year, Arnold returned to the U.S. and entered Dallas Theological Seminary for studies in Hebrew

and Old Testament. He also began working as a missionary with ABMJ (today, Chosen People Ministries).

Jacob Parash
http://www.moriel.org

Jacob is a Hebrew-speaking evangelist to the Jews and a Bible teacher elaborating on the original Judeo-Christian background and hermeneutics of the New Testament, and his emphasis is on church planting and missions. He and Moriel have also been a conservative voice for biblically-based discernment among moderate Pentecostals and Charismatics opposed to the seductions of the ecumenism, money oriented preaching and hype artistry, "charismania" and psycho-babble prevalent in today's church.

Jacob and Moriel are committed to the conviction that we are in the Last Days approaching the return of Christ and that contemporary events in the Middle East, the moral deterioration of society, the destruction of the environment, the globalization of the world economy, the rise of a pseudo-democratic federal Europe and, above all, the apostasy in the contemporary church, are all events of prophetic significance eschatologically.

Bibles, Language and study materials

This is by no means an exhaustive list but these resources are ones that I use on a regular basis. The Internet is full of resources but I would use them with caution since anyone can put anything on the web true or not. If you have resources that are not listed I would be grateful if you would let me know via email at ekklasea@worldsofwonderpublishing.com.

Translations:

The Amplified Bible - Zondervan Publishing

The International Standard Bible - The ISV Foundation Committee on Translation

The Wuest Expanded Translation - Kenneth S. Wuest
Publisher: William B. Eerdmans Publishing Company

The King James version of course.

I suggest that ***no one ever use*** paraphrased bibles since they are prone to the bias and errors of the paraphraser. Why not start with something that is a least closer to the original thought. If you need a version that is written in a modern style English try the International Standard Version
(Not the New International Standard NIV -   which has numerous errors and omissions)

Word Studies:

Word Studies from the Greek New Testament (4 volume set) [Hardcover] by Kenneth S. Wuest Publisher: William B. Eerdmans Publishing Company

Vincent's Word Studies in the New Testament (4 Volume Set) Hardcover – by M. R. Vincent Publisher: Hendrickson Publishers

Word Pictures in the New Testament (6 Volumes) [Hardcover] by A. T. Robertson - Publisher: Holman Reference

Hebrew and Greek Words Dictionary

Vine's Complete Expository Dictionary of Old and New Testament Words: With Topical Index by W. E. Vine Publisher: Thomas Nelson

The New Strong's Complete Dictionary of Bible Words by James Strong Publisher: Thomas Nelson

Mounce's Complete Expository Dictionary of Old and New Testament Words by William D. Mounce Publisher: Zondervan

Thayer's Greek-English Lexicon of the New Testament: by Joseph Thayer Publisher: Hendrickson Publishers

Complete Word Study Dictionary: New Testament
(Word Study Series) by Dr. Spiros Zodhiates
Publisher: AMG Publishers

Complete Word Study Dictionary: Old Testament
(Word Study Series) Hardcover by Warren Baker

New Testament Greek To Hebrew Dictionary
by Jeff A. Benner Publisher: Virtualbookworm.com Publishing

The Ancient Hebrew Lexicon of the Bible
Jeff A. Benner Virtualbookworm.com Publishing

Bible Software:

Some of these resources are available on your phone and can easily be taken wherever you go. I have the Amplified, Wuest's Expanded translation, the International Standard, the King James and the New King James all on my phone along with many of the resources I have mentioned.

Wordsearch - by Lifeway - Available for Personal Computers, iPad, and smart phones.

Olive Tree - Available for Personal Computers, iPad, and smart phones.

The Word - theword.net Costas Stergiou- Available for Personal Computers. At this writing I am not aware of an iPad or smart phone app.

e-Sword - Rick Meyers

Interlinear Scripture analyzer for Greek and Hebrew.
André de Mol.

Blue Letter Bible - on-line Bible search utility with multiple versions and Strong's numbers with Vines Expository New Testament Greek.
http://www.blueletterbible.org/

Made in the USA
Middletown, DE
04 December 2014